# NAILED IT!

## HOW ONE WOMAN TURNED A
## DREAM BUSINESS INTO A HUGE SUCCESS

*Jeanette Sklivanou*

# R<sup>e</sup>think

First published in Great Britain in 2022 by Rethink Press
(www.rethinkpress.com)

# Contents

# Timeline

**2009** – Greece suffers from a huge financial crash. The Sklivanou family property development business fails.

**2010** – Jeanette begins to think of new business ideas and starts a small children's spa party company. She approaches an American nail polish company to ask to become their distributor in Greece. They say no.

**2011** – The idea of Snails – derived from 'safe nails' – is born, registered under the company name Safe 'N' Beautiful (S'N'B). Jeanette spends months finding a factory to make washable nail polish and makes her first order.

**2012** – Jeanette introduces S'N'B to a beauty expo in London and Dubai. Ten countries including Dubai, Qatar, France and Russia agree to distribute Snails. S'N'B wins the Mumpreneur Gold website award.

**2013** – Snails takes on its first employees and moves from Jeanette's kitchen to an office and warehouse. Ralph Lauren asks Snails products to appear in their Milan show.

**2014** – Snails wins the bronze Greek Exports award. The S'N'B wash-off range for adults is released. Snails wins the Tillywig Toy 'Parents' favourite product' award.

**2015** – The biggest year yet. Hachette makes a massive order to sell Snails nail polish. S'N'B buys a bottle-filling machine. Sales increase more than four-fold and Snails products are now sold in over forty-five countries.

**2016** – Snails expands their office to an additional floor to keep up with demand.

**2017** – S'N'B products are sold in over seventy countries, mainly by toy and children's product distributors. The new S'N'BIO range is released, made from vegetable dyes. Snails launches the world's first vitamin- and rose-water-infused nail polish aimed at teenagers.

**2018** – Partnership with Götz, a German toy manu-facturer to make a doll and nail polish package. New S'N'B product releases include body and hair glitter and hair chalk. S'N'B wins the Preferred Choice award. Top Lithuanian children's TV show *Super Experts* votes Snails as the best and safest product of the year.

**2019** – Snails wins three awards at the Greek Exports Awards – two gold (top innovation in exports and top export packaging) and one silver (top branded export product). Snails is sold in KaDeWe, the German equivalent of Harrods, with a fifteen-square-foot retail space. The Snails eye shadow cake is launched.

**2021** – The Snails range is expanded to include jewellery range Charmed. S'N'B wins a Global Green Beauty award, a Parents' Picks award and Mums Choice award. Snails opens a fifteen-square-foot retail space inside Hamleys on Regent Street, London – the oldest and largest toy shop in the world. Snails also starts selling in FAO Schwarz, in the Rockefeller Center, New York.

**2022** – A new social media marketing campaign is launched. Jeanette writes *Nailed It!* More products are in development. Watch this space!

# Introduction

I kept blinking to make sure I had read the email correctly.

Ralph Lauren. *The* Ralph Lauren?

I read the message several times over.

*Ralph Lauren Europe would like a nail polish from the Snails children's collection to feature in a Milan catwalk photo shoot.*

I sat back in my chair, laughing, absorbing the incredible news. For the past three years, I had worked tirelessly, developing and selling a brand of quality children's nail polish. It had begun as something I had only dared to imagine.

I wanted Safe-Nails, known as Snails, to one day be viewed alongside household-name designer brands like Chanel. In my mind, there was no reason a children's product couldn't be recognised as a luxury brand alongside the best in the world. And now Ralph Lauren was asking to feature a sample of Snails in their prestigious show! This moment was one to savour. It proved to me anything is possible and with hard work and dedication, any dream can come true, however big it is.

I knew nothing about the cosmetics industry when I started, but that didn't stop me from believing I could make my business a success. I learned everything by Googling or asking others for advice, though at the beginning, very often people refused my requests for help. Many people, including my own family and friends, were doubtful when I told them I wanted to set up a business selling children's nail polish.

'Why do you think a luxury nail polish for kids will sell, when we have families starving in this country?' asked one concerned friend. On the face of it, she was right. I started work on Safe 'N' Beautiful following a huge financial crisis in my country of Greece, when over 500,000 people had to flee to find work. Our family property business had collapsed. My husband was depressed, and my kids faced losing their schooling. During such a desperate and miserable time, was this really the opportune moment to start a business aimed at painting kids' nails?

But I believed in the idea enough to take the risk. I am half Greek and half English, born to a Greek father and an English mother. Unless we sold everything and went to live with my mum's family in the UK, we had to find a new way to make a livelihood.

My first idea was to open a small children's spa party business – the first one in Greece. It worked quite successfully and put food on our table but after a year or so, I realised this business wasn't going to work long term. It was time consuming and didn't bring in much money. Yet it had given me a shot of confidence. Perhaps now I could try something else and build a cosmetic business that would turn over more profit and make a real impact. I also didn't want to rely solely on the Greek market following the crash. I wanted to sell a product internationally with the potential to grow.

It was then that I came up with the idea of children's washable nail polish and Safe 'N' Beautiful (S'N'B) was born.

For anyone who is starting a business, especially women, the obstacles are massive and sometimes appear insurmountable. The cosmetics industry is notoriously competitive and every year, thousands of new products try and fail to make the grade. Finding a unique selling point and developing a successful brand is a challenge. I have written this book to help. Within these pages, we will explore everything you need to know when it comes to starting a business:

- How to think of a good idea

- How to develop it

- How to keep going when you feel like giving up

- And most of all, how to *succeed*

I believe any woman can become an entrepreneur if she wants to. I'm writing this book not to brag about my success, but to share my journey with Snails in detail, to reveal how it was done. After all, if I can do it, so can you.

# ONE
# The Beginning

There is, according to Sophia Amoruso – the woman behind the global brand Nasty Gal – two types of entrepreneurs: those who want to become one and those who have to.[1] I was in the latter category. In 2009, when my family's business collapsed, things weren't just bad. They were *really* bad. If there was a rock bottom, this was it.

I had spent many years working in our successful family business in Athens, Greece, where we bought land and built flats. After my husband completed the building work, I managed the interior design. Alongside this, I looked after our home and young daughters. Our flourishing company paid for our comfortable lifestyle,

---

1.   S Amoruso, #*GIRLBOSS* (Penguin, 2015)

where we could afford a lovely house and send our daughters to an English-speaking international school.

Then suddenly, almost overnight, we had flats we couldn't sell due to the financial crisis. Within weeks we went from a prosperous family to one facing awful dilemmas we had never anticipated. My husband plunged into depression and we were filled with worries every day about how we could survive. Despite feeling low myself, I tried my best to shield our two daughters from the worst of it. I never spoke about money worries around them, even if I knew our savings couldn't last.

But during this time of extreme uncertainty, something unexpected happened to me. Fresh ideas formed in my mind about what to do next. The future was blank and I had to fill it with something new, so I started to think of possibilities that had never crossed my mind before. I also thought of this saying I had once read: 'Two things define you. Your patience when you have nothing and your attitude when you have everything.'

That dark period of my life turned out to be an advantage for me for two reasons. First, having everything taken away created head space and time to think. I wasn't busy helping to sell flats anymore, so I had more hours in the day to consider our options. Second, from rock bottom there was only one way to go, and that was up again.

# The gift of desperation

As I was feeling more open-minded to ideas and concepts, I began to read more, and I came across *The Secret* by Rhonda Byrne.[2] This seminal self-help book is based on the belief that thoughts can directly change a person's life. Suddenly I felt like my eyes had been opened. The compelling stories in the book made me feel energised in a way I hadn't experienced before.

There were many lines from the book that leaped out at me, but my favourite was this: 'There is no such thing as a hopeless situation. Every single circumstance of your life can change!'

This was exactly what I needed to read. Instead of feeling completely negative about the future and seeing it as a black hole, I was overwhelmed with a renewed sense that anything is possible. I saw my abilities in a different light. It wasn't just an abstract idea that I could start a successful business. I decided it was *going* to happen.

I don't believe in magic. I am not religious or superstitious. But I do know that I was looking for direction in my life and reading this book gave me something to hold on to. The power of these words worked. I knew, if I put my mind to something now, I could do it.

---

2.   R Byrne, *The Secret* (Simon & Schuster, 2008)

## Backing ideas with self-belief

Self-belief is the single most important ingredient for any entrepreneur. Although I didn't yet know what my business would be, I started to think of ideas.

During a visit to family in the UK that summer, my nieces attended a kids' spa party, something I'd never come across before. The little girls were treated as if they were visiting a real spa – they had their toenails painted, were given face masks and were brought drinks on a tray. It looked like enormous fun and I knew my daughters, aged six and eleven, who loved playing grown-ups, would have enjoyed it too.

At this point, the only place to take kids for a party experience in Greece was at a soft play centre, and this was very expensive. I had done it once and it had cost over 1,000 euros. This certainly wasn't affordable for most people, or indeed, something you could do every year, especially in the poor economic climate.

With no spa parties on offer in Greece, I knew there was a gap in the market, and it was an original idea. This was reason enough to persuade me to try it out. Although our country was going through the worst economic crisis in centuries, with businesses everywhere going bust and people facing poverty and starvation, as a mother, I was desperate to shield my children from the horrors of what was happening in the outside world. I still wanted to treat them for their birthdays and make these occasions feel special in whatever way I could, even if it meant spending my last penny. And if I felt like this, I guessed other Greek mothers would feel the same way.

*This is an important point – if you can think of a product idea that fills a gap in your own life, chances are it will fill a gap in other people's lives too.*

I chose the name Kids Spa Parties, set about making a Facebook page (which is free), put together a simple website (for a small fee) and ordered some fun and child-friendly products I found online. I made a chocolate face mask using cocoa, honey and oatmeal, and used juice for child 'champagne'. I also made some pink dressing gowns with motifs of Kids Spa Parties and bought flip-flops and hair-bands. It was professional-looking despite being DIY, because I paid attention to detail. I spent our savings on these products, ignoring my husband's warnings that it could be a waste of money.

My idea was for little girls to feel pampered in a fun spa setting that we would bring to their homes, so there was no need to pay for a venue. We offered different packages and charged a maximum of 400 euros for the gold package for fifteen girls. If I was being honest, I had no idea myself if this would work, but I was willing to try.

My hunch was right. Kids Spa Parties took off. We even had enough bookings to employ two manicurists to paint the kids' nails.

It wasn't because people suddenly had lots of money that the business succeeded. It was because instinct had correctly told me that mothers like me were prepared to go without for their kids. Even those who did have spare cash wanted to use it wisely and we were a company who provided great value for money, especially if you compared us to competitors, like the soft play place that charged over twice as much.

I was so relieved. The first few bookings didn't bring in huge revenue, but they gave us enough money to put food on the table and pay for all our basic necessities at home.

## Taking chances and dealing with rejection

It was during this hectic period that I first came across child-friendly nail varnish. The product I was using was sold by a company in America, so I had to pay import fees. It was a surprise to me that you couldn't buy children's nail polish *anywhere* in Europe.

With my new-found confidence, I took a chance and emailed the American company and filled out a questionnaire to become a distributor for them in Europe. One question asked how I would expand the business in my country. I went into a lot of detail about how I would present the brand at a Greek exhibition. I even wrote down what colours and props I would use on my stall. Unbelievably, two years later, they used the exact exhibition ideas I had suggested – but at that time, I received a negative reply to my offer.

Undeterred, I called them on the phone. 'I would love to distribute your nail polish in Greece,' I said.

'Have you any experience in the cosmetics industry?' asked the lady, the tone of her voice edged with cynicism.

I admitted I didn't, but explained I ran a new small independent children's spa party business. 'And I have lots of enthusiasm,' I assured her, 'and access to a market of little girls who love nail polish.'

I heard a small sigh. 'Without any relevant experience, we cannot ask you to distribute,' came the blunt reply. Then she put the phone down.

I was taken aback. How could I get experience if I was never given a chance? It was a big blow, but I tried to put my disappointment aside and focus on the positives of my little business.

As I look back, every time I thought I was being rejected from something good, I was actually being redirected to something better. Products are born every day in real life by simple people. All you need to do is sit and observe. What do people need? What is missing? We have all said at some point in our lives, 'I wish such-and-such product existed...'

## Turning ideas into reality

To my complete shock, my small business attracted a lot of free publicity in the local press, so I was able to afford to give out flyers in stores and schools and had a small advert on the radio to publicise it further. Then a researcher for the Greek news evening programme contacted me. They wanted to interview me on TV!

This felt surreal. What had begun as a tiny local business was now making national news headlines. The business was still not a big earner, but it proved something to me. *Within a few months, I had taken an idea in my head and had turned it into a business that had made the national news.* This incredible experience showed the powerful suggestions in *The Secret* were true. With dedication, hard work, an open mind and, most importantly, self-belief, you can turn an idea from thin air into a tangible success.

For eighteen months, Kids Spa Parties did well, but we faced unexpected challenges. I received critical emails demanding to know why I was forcing little girls to 'grow up too soon' with make-up and pampering. I didn't agree with this opinion. Boys play with guns pretending to be at war, but we don't accuse them of growing up too soon. We see it as an innocent game. For little girls, playing with make-up is the same as face paint. At some point, every girl pretends to play mummy, and this is an innocent extension of this.

I ignored these emails and focused on remaining positive. We still had so many good reviews and I knew we were bringing joy to kids' lives. But I was keen to learn more about the cosmetics industry. I set about Googling what cosmetic products make the most money. Far and away, the most profitable was nail varnish.

This led me to the next good idea that would change my life.

---

### QUESTIONS TO INSPIRE IDEAS FOR A BUSINESS

- What are your hobbies and interests?
- What are your favourite products?
- Is there a product you need in your life?
- In a dream world, what would you like to invent?

---

## TWO

# The Big Brainstorm

Allowing time and space for your ideas to flow is essential. We can easily fill up daylight hours with screen time, household tasks and worries until there is no time left to think of anything outside of the box. To think of a creative business idea, we must slow things down in our daily lives for new ideas to form.

Watching my daughters play with the American kids' nail varnish was what gave me the light bulb moment for Snails. The imported nail polish needed acetone to remove it, and as my kids sat painting their nails one afternoon on the sofa, I couldn't take my eyes off them.

I was worried they would spill it. I didn't know whether we had enough nail polish remover for them to clean their nails afterwards. I was concerned about what it would do to their skin. And I really didn't like the smell of it! I couldn't relax and let them play without hovering over them like a helicopter.

'I wish there was a nail varnish for children where I didn't need to worry about spillages,' I thought, eyeing my daughters' messy play. And there, I had said the magic words: 'I wish'.

A tsunami of questions struck me:

- Why isn't children's nail polish washable?
- Could nail varnish be completely non-toxic?
- Why isn't there a child-friendly nail varnish made in Europe?
- Why is children's nail varnish so cheap-looking?
- Could there be a high-end children's nail polish?

All of these questions struck a chord with me as a mum and, again, I knew it would with other mothers too. It was then I had my plan. I would make a washable luxury nail polish designed especially for children and have it made in Europe.

## What experience do you need to start your business?

None. Zilch. Nothing. Think of how many people in the world would love to follow a business dream but believe they lack the experience to do it. The truth is, *anything* in life can be learned, especially when it comes to being an entrepreneur. With the internet at our fingertips, we have access to a wealth of information and we can research any topic we like. We can also teach ourselves things via YouTube or by reading articles.

There are other ingredients to starting a business that are more important than knowledge or experience. These include:

- Belief in your product
- Time
- Belief in yourself
- Research

Let's take a look at each of these.

## Belief in your product

Without complete belief in your idea, you will never get it off the ground. I completely believed in my product idea from day one and you must too. You can't keep changing your ideas. You must stick to one and run with it.

## Time

Without experience, you must be prepared to put in the hours to learn what you need to know. Long working days, overtime, weekends, evenings – it's going to be tough. There's no short cut to get around the long hours. But you will have breakthroughs and find wonderful people along the way who will help things work more smoothly or quickly at times.

## Belief in yourself

This can be the most challenging factor. Digging deep and finding extra energy for self-belief is necessary. Some women naturally struggle to believe in their abilities, but after my revelations reading *The Secret*, I understood I had to believe in myself for others to believe in my product.

## Research, research, research

You can't ever do enough research when it comes to the product you're considering making. When I began researching nail polish, I tried to leave no topic uncovered. First, I discovered nail polish was consistently a best-selling cosmetic item. It had enduring appeal and made the most money out of all cosmetic products on sale. I read that, after mascara, nail polish is the most popular form of make-up in the world, and the market was still growing and wasn't likely to decrease in the future.

Next, I looked up brands I admired. OPI was the number-one nail varnish brand in the world in 2010. I loved the branding, the attention to detail with lovely solid bottles, and the array of colours.

I've always been fascinated by women who founded their own companies. When I started out, I read about the American brand essie and was drawn to the story of Essie Weingarten, who started work on her dream in 1981.[3] She began her business in her garage, choosing twelve shades and selling them directly to salons. Thirty years later, her company was sold for millions to L'Oréal. Her story was a huge inspiration to me. Until then, it had never occurred to me that an ordinary woman without experience in the cosmetics industry would be capable of such success, but she was proof it was.

I took my research seriously. I wanted to know for sure that the product I was choosing to throw all of my time, energy and belief behind was likely to succeed. I printed out all the articles I read and filed them to refer back to. At this point, all knowledge was power.

The places I looked at while conducting my research included:

- Leading newspapers and magazines in the USA and UK, including *The New Yorker, The Times, The Economist,* and other broadsheet papers

---

3. www.essie.com/about-us, accessed 24 June 2022

and specialist magazines. These are useful for background research and to spot latest trends.

- Google. I would put in 'nail polish economy' and look at every single thing that came up, scrolling through to spot anything interesting.

- My own experience. I considered what was important to me and the people I knew – my daughters, my friends, and the Kids Spa Parties business. I made notes of my own and other people's comments on products.

- Other successful people's stories. The memoirs and business books of those you admire can be a wealth of information and inspiration.

Around this time, I also read Steve Jobs' biography by Walter Isaacson.[4] His personal story created a lasting impression. Here was a simple, humble man who didn't go to Harvard or Yale, nor did he come from a business background, but he still made it. I have never liked people who show off their wealth or status and was drawn to how he kept his humility despite his success.

The personal stories of Essie Weingarten and Steve Jobs made me realise everyone has a chance of making it. They came up with an original idea, worked incredibly hard and never stopped believing in themselves – and I could do that too.

---

4. W Isaacson, *Steve Jobs: The exclusive biography* (Abacus, 2015)

# Big questions to consider

## 1. What are your existing skill sets?

If we don't have direct experience, it's easy to think we don't have the necessary skills. I didn't know anything about nail polish – what it is made from, who makes it, where to buy bottles, anything about marketing or branding. The list was endless. I didn't even know how the product ends up in a store. I had no idea how distributors worked. But that didn't mean I couldn't teach myself or find out the information I needed online.

Meanwhile, I chose to focus on the skills I did have, such as:

- My insights as a mother. I knew my market, because I was the target market and a typical customer.

- My experience with design. I had studied graphic design during my interior design course at university, and this helped with packaging and product ideas.

- My drive and optimism. I loved make-up and playing with my daughters and had a product idea I was passionate about.

- My hard work ethic. As a mother who had worked for our family company, I knew how to manage my time and juggle personal and work commitments.

- My people skills. From my own spa business, I was used to dealing with clients face-to-face. I was good at customer service and already worked with consumers of the children's cosmetics market.

Skills such as dedication, curiosity about life and the ability to communicate are just as important (if not more) than actual experience. You can develop your experience as you go, which will add to the life skills you already have.

## 2. What gap will your product fill in the marketplace?

Once you've thought of an idea for a possible product, now you need to know:

- Does the product already exist?

- If it does, could you do it better or differently?

For example, there were a few other children's nail polishes available, but none were washable or made in Europe, and none of them were luxury branded. They were cheap and throwaway. Many also contained harsh ingredients not suitable for young skin.

There was no magic place I discovered this. I simply Googled the information and spent hours making notes.

## 3. What is unique about your idea?

Of the hundreds of thousands of new products that are released every year, only a handful will succeed. But what makes the difference between a success and failure?

One big factor is the product's USP, its unique selling point. *There is no point in trying to copy what is already out there.* Ask yourself this: 'What problem does my product solve?'

Think of any successful household product and it almost always solves a problem, often making household tasks or life easier. For example, an electric toothbrush makes toothbrushing easier and faster. A dishwasher saves time and water on cleaning. A detangling brush for kids makes brushing hair less painful. A make-up subscription package delivering items to the door makes trying cosmetics a convenient novelty.

Popular products tackle specific problems such as:

1. **Saving people money.** For example, a high-quality face cream of which only small quantities are needed means the customer buys less in the long-term.

2. **Making life more enjoyable.** Snails does this! Kids can now have fun with nail polish but with none of the parental stress of worrying they will

spill it on furnishings or that it will be hard or damaging to take off.

3. **Preventing future worse problems.** For example, a product that promises to help a consumer in the future, such as toothpaste that rebuilds tooth enamel, meaning they make fewer trips to the dentist, or a cosmetic product that is refillable, allowing them to cut down on wasteful packaging.

# Further considerations

## Consumer trends

Looking at consumer trends is important. What is popular right now? This is not to say you should copy an existing product, but to look at what makes that product successful. Sometimes it's possible to go against the grain, but often new products follow trends in the market.

For example, sustainability is an ongoing trend demanded by most environmentally aware customers today. This aided my own thinking when I had to make decisions about packaging. I decided I would make all my packaging biodegradable and the bottles recyclable.

## Where your product is made

When it comes to any product, there are certain regions of the world that excel in manufacturing to an excellent standard, and this is something both consumers and distributors look out for. For example, Italy is well regarded for glassware, Germany for mechanical goods, like cars, and Japan for quality technology.

When it comes to cosmetics, France is viewed as the leading country that manufactures quality products. This is where Snails is made and it is something we're very proud of. I was reluctant to attempt to make our product in Greece, not only because of the criticism I mentioned earlier about providing cosmetics for girls, but also because of the lack of infrastructure for making the product. There were no factories I could order the ingredients or buy the bottles from. At the beginning of my journey, it wasn't worth my time even trying to change this.

## The cost

Of course, at the beginning, we have to consider start-up costs too. And you will want to minimise them. Some people call this a bootstrap approach, paying minimal costs and doing most of the legwork yourself. This is what I did. I was lucky enough to have the savings to kick-start my business, but other ways of securing funding are possible.

It's always good to consider what you can afford right at the start. Do you need a loan? Does your bank offer business loans at good rates of interest? How much will initial product costs be? What are the profit margins? What money will you need to attend expos to find distributors?

I found writing a list of everything I was capable of doing myself helped me. For example, I could do the research, find the factory where to make the product, look up some distributors, and think about branding and design. It was a huge amount, and would take thousands of hours, but I had the internet to help me.

There are some things I don't recommend skimping on, such as a decent, efficient, professionally designed website and packaging. I'll go into detail about these later in the section on finance.

## Spreading the risk

Every start-up entrepreneur takes a risk, with one in five new businesses failing in the first year of operation,[5] but you can spread that risk, which I did.

I wanted to create a product that I wasn't going to sell in Greece alone. This was because of the economic

---

5.  G McIntyre, 'What percentage of small businesses fail? (And other need-to-know stats)', Fundera, 20 November 2020, www.fundera .com/blog/what-percentage-of-small-businesses-fail, accessed 26 May 2022

collapse. I needed to avoid relying on the unstable market of our home country. I also wished to reach other markets in the world who didn't take the attitude that wearing nail polish forced kids to grow up too soon. I set out to sell my product in countries whose parents would embrace the idea, not recoil from it.

I decided to target the European market. Not only would this spread the risk, but also all European buyers were having to pay import fees on nail polish from America, so the opportunity to buy a product made in Europe would be attractive to them.

But I didn't want to consider this a done deal. If, for whatever reason, the European market didn't work out, I wanted to try the Middle Eastern market and even the American market too. Thinking globally from the start gave me a vision to work towards.

---

## CASE STUDY: LUCY ROUT, TABUU

Lucy Rout is the founder of Tabuu, a new start-up that makes sustainable and fashionable-looking pill boxes. Lucy came up with the idea for her business because she couldn't find a pill box on the market that she liked, so she invented one. This is her story:

When I was twenty-five, I survived pancreatic cancer and afterwards had to take twenty pills per day. The only pill boxes I could find were clunky, oversized plastic cases that looked like they were designed for the elderly. I wanted a fashionable pill case that looked pleasing and was also environmentally friendly. But I couldn't find one anywhere.

My big dream was to design a product that would help build a world where people can choose their accessories to suit their needs and not feel stigmatised by disability or illness. I want a pill box people did not feel embarrassed about pulling out of their handbag.

I knew nothing about making pill boxes and had to learn everything from scratch, via YouTube or Google. I used my own savings at first, and used as many things for free as possible. I even used a free trial of Photoshop for my initial logo designs.

Eventually, I found a factory that made pill boxes and sent my ideas. Once I had a prototype made, I ordered more, opened a website and started selling on Amazon. The order rate was huge right from the start. I knew there would be other people like me who wanted a lovely pill case to keep their medication, and it turned out there were many!

Retailers are also catching up with this demand. I thought it would take years before Tabuu attracted the eye of distributors, but I am already in talks with major retailers and pharmacies. They acknowledge the need for the market to be more inclusive.

## TOP TIPS FOR BUILDING ON YOUR INITIAL IDEAS

- Belief in yourself and your product idea is more important than lack of knowledge or experience at this stage.

- Google is your friend and can fill many gaps in your knowledge.

- Establish your financial position early so you can focus on making your idea a reality.

- Spread financial and market risk to increase your chances of success once you get going.

# THREE
# Action Stations

Ideas are all well and good, but it's taking action that moves things forward. The first 'action' you need to take is establishing your belief in your product and idea completely from day one. You have to be passionate about your potential product, because you're going to have to sell it to other people. This point is vital. As Steve Jobs said, 'If you're not passionate enough from the start, you'll never stick it out.'[6]

## Immediate goals

Once you're sure this is the product for you, it's time to kick off the action plan. On day one, I simply carried on

---

6. M Steren, 'Follow Your Passion', Medium, 23 February 2018, https:// medium.com/@marc_steren/you-have-to-be-burning-with-an-idea -or-a-problem-or-a-wrong-that-you-want-to-right-882e4303fb0d, accessed 24 June 2022

Googling. My first challenge was to find out everything there was to know about nail varnish – where it was made, what it was made out of, who made nail varnish in Europe. I went down a rabbit hole of information and made pages of notes.

I discovered that most of the good manufacturers could not be found online and that the best way to find contact details was via expos. Luckily, I found one number online and that led me to others. Having covered the basics, I set about thinking about my next steps. I knew if this idea was to succeed, I had to sound professional. I had no company yet, nor experience, but I could communicate what I wanted and planned to ask for that repeatedly.

At this stage, my immediate achievable goals were:

1. Find out the number of factories that make nail varnish.
2. Ring them all and ask whether they make different nail varnish formulas and whether they could make a washable formula.
3. Find someone who will say yes to making the nail varnish I want.

## The importance of goals

Having a list of definable goals will spur on the initial first steps. And when you take these actions, remember they don't have to be perfect or get immediate results. I learned on the job. I had no expertise in what I was doing, but I kept doing it. As Ann Handley put it in her International Women's Day article for IBM, 'Be an amateur. Not everything you do has to be good, especially at first.'[7]

What worked for me was writing down a 'mega list' of overall things to do and then breaking this down into a 'micro list' of daily tasks. I was filled with enthusiasm and I had a deadline in my mind. Any batches of nail polish I ordered would expire within two years and the savings I had in the bank wouldn't even last that long. Time was not on my side.

While still trying to find a factory to make the product, I started thinking about the brand, the name, what would be on my company website, etc. I settled on the name 'Safe 'N' Beautiful' for the company and 'Safe-Nails' for the product. I wanted something simple for people to remember and something parents would be attracted by. I wrote it down in a notebook and made a list of my next goals.

When starting a new business, there are thousands of different tasks and components to keep on top of. The key is to make the actions manageable and not

7.  A Handley, 'Career advice on International Women's Day: 4 things I'd do again, 2 mistakes I made', LinkedIn, 8 March 2017, www .linkedin.com/pulse/career-advice-international-womens-day -4-things-id-do-ann-handley, accessed 26 May 2022

overwhelming. If I had told myself, 'I want to set up a kids' nail varnish empire to rival Chanel as soon as possible', I would have been totally overawed at the idea. Keeping the actions smaller made them more achievable. Writing down goals also helps to chart your progress and keep you accountable. When you cross off a goal on your list, you'll feel good about things moving forward. It will show you the progress you're making over the days, weeks and months, which is important for your own morale.

Even when I was rejected by a voice at the end of a phone in a factory, I kept stock of who I had spoken to and when. I might have been dismissed by a stranger on the phone, but I had achieved my own task and told myself I was one step closer to finding someone who would one day say yes.

## Understand you cannot do this alone

It was Helen Keller who said, 'Alone we can do so little. Together we can do so much.'[8] You can think of a good idea alone, but you will need other people to help make your dream product work. There is no way around this. Everything you see in the world involves the effort of a team behind the scenes.

The big issue to accept at this stage is that in the early days of any company being built, most people will

---

8.  JP Lash, *Helen and Teacher: The story of Helen Keller and Anne Sullivan Macy* (Delacorte Press/Seymour Lawrence, 1980, p489)

not want to help. The majority of people are too busy with their day-to-day jobs and don't have the time or inclination to give to a person, often a stranger, without experience and whom they do not know. This is human nature. When you share your ideas and dreams, most people will expect you to fail and not want to waste their precious time helping. Expect this and don't allow rejection to put you off doing what you need to do.

Let me share what happened to me. I found phone numbers for factories in America, Italy, the UK and two cosmetic companies in Greece. Cosmetics is not something my country specialises in. In fact, Greece's main exports are olive oil and feta cheese, so I really was trying something unique. But undaunted, I contacted one of the Greek companies to ask them for help, because they had a factory with a production line.

Surely, I believed, they would have an interest in my brilliant idea, if only just a faint one. But this is how the conversation went:

'Do you produce nail polish?' I asked.

'Yes,' they said.

'Is it possible for you to make a washable formula suitable for children?' I asked.

The voice laughed. 'No.'

End of discussion.

I would be lying if I said this wasn't a blow. There wasn't enough interest in my product to even speak about it. No intrigue, no curiosity, absolutely nothing but ridicule.

In moments like this, we have to shake off the inevitably creeping sense of failure or doubt. I would take a short break – go for a walk, talk to a friend, or inspire myself by reading a book written by someone successful. The most compelling stories in memoirs are ones of overcoming failure. The only difference between an entrepreneur who failed and one who succeeded is that the one who succeeded never gave up.

## Keep on keeping on

I hardened my resolve and continued calling the other factories on my list. I got the same response each time.

'No, sorry.'

'No, I cannot help.'

'No, I do not know.'

'No, this is not our specialism.'

Once again, I had to take a step back and look at the bigger picture. Hearing 'no' over and over again is horrible, even if you totally believe in yourself. But the more noes I heard, the more I told myself to be determined to hear a yes. I promised myself when – not if – it happened, it would feel even better after so much rejection.

It's never going to be easy, and if people keep saying no, you have to keep going regardless. Some might say my success came because I got lucky, that it was a fluke. I thought of it as a numbers game and knew that eventually, someone would be willing to give me their time.

It was a person who answered the phone in a UK factory who unexpectedly helped me out.

'I would like to make a nail polish for children that is washable,' I repeated for the umpteenth time.

'Uh?' came the reply, which was better than the usual 'No!'

Viewing the pause as an opportunity, I explained I needed something washable and water based.

'OK. So you need this formula for yourself? Do you need a big supply?' he asked.

It was my turn to say no then. I knew I needed the smallest order possible. That was all I could afford. I still hadn't worked out the costs and profit margins were still something I was learning about.

'You need another factory based in Paris,' the man said. 'I can pass you on the number.'

If I could have reached down the phone and hugged him, I would have done. This was my first turning point. Without the kind person who happened to pick up the phone that day in the UK factory, I wouldn't be where I am now. God bless him.

## The first big break

I took a deep breath and called the number of the French factory. Luckily, the person at the end of the phone spoke English.

'Can you make a washable children's nail varnish?' I asked.

They paused and then said the magic word. 'Yes.'

'What is the minimum order quantity?' I said, barely able to breathe with anticipation.

'Twenty-five kilos.'

'That would be perfect!' I almost cried.

Incredibly, this factory had the capability of making washable children's nail polish but nobody had ever asked them to do it before. I asked for their list of ingredients and they provided it. It made little sense to me, I had never heard of any of the components, but I duly wrote them down and did my research.

Once again, Google and a pad and pen were my friends. I looked up each ingredient, checking out statistics for how safe it was, what it was made from, was it cancerous. I already knew the American company claimed their products were free of three different toxins: dibutyl phthalate (DBP), formaldehyde and toluene. I asked the French factory if they could guarantee the same for my product.

The product they made was already free of those toxins, and in fact, they were free of three more, including formaldehyde resin, parabens and camphor. Now my product could be free of six toxins and so 'six free'. I could already be ahead of my competition.

The next step was to choose colours I liked and the factory would make up batches. Then I needed to find bottles to fill. All of a sudden, my idea was becoming very real.

## My muses

Having a muse really helps keep motivation levels high when you start any business. I was fortunate in that my daughters were my muses. I decided I would run all my ideas past them to get a child's-eye view of my product. I had two little girls who were my target market, so it made sense. And even to this day, I do not make a single decision about S'N'B products without their input.

When the first shade samples of the basic colours arrived from the factory, I showed the girls and asked them what they thought. They loved them. To my surprise, they loved the colour green, so I included this in the initial collection. Already, I was learning from them, because I wouldn't have included that shade myself.

Having a trusted circle of people whom you can run ideas past is worth everything at this early stage of your business. There will be things that you're not able to see or have not experienced, which can limit your understanding. Getting a second and third opinion is extremely worthwhile.

---

## CASE STUDY: SHALOM LLOYD, NATURALLY TRIBAL

Qualified pharmacist Shalom Lloyd had no experience in the cosmetic industry when she set up her British skincare company, Naturally Tribal, in 2016.

After her son was born, Shalom looked for natural alternatives to help treat his eczema. Eventually, this led to her creating products made in the UK with ingredients from Africa. The company makes scrubs, oils, washes and moisturisers. This is Shalom's story:

I was a nerdy scientist who found myself trying to make it in the beauty industry and I was a fish out of water. I believed in my products enough to remortgage my house to help finance the start-up, but not necessarily in myself and my ability to take my products to market. Self-doubt and imposter syndrome weighed me down. Although I was a successful woman in the pharmaceutical industry, what on earth made me think I could conquer the skincare world?

I had to get over myself, and a turning point came when our company was selected as a Commonwealth Export Champion unexpectedly. As part of our selection, we had the opportunity to approach experienced business people to act as our mentors. I spotted John Mohin OBE, who was a top executive from Wedgwood, and asked for his help. To my surprise, he loved our business model and later said, 'I see you as the Estée Lauder of Africa.'

John taught me to see myself how others do – a woman who deserves to be sitting at the table of other SMEs, making her business a success. Today, I also mentor other women in the science and health care industries and as a Cherie Blair mentor. The importance of others when you are on a journey to make a business succeed is everything.

I wish I had mastered communication and people skills earlier in life. Involving the right people in my idea from the start would have saved me a lot of pain. But going through this process has taught me some valuable life lessons. If I could go back and give myself some advice, it would be: You'll be OK.

Just take your time. Don't succumb to the pressure, surround yourself with the right people, don't be afraid to say no, and place more value on your time.

## QUESTIONS FOR WHEN THE ACTION BEGINS

- **What are your immediate goals?** Rate them as long term and short term. What do you need to do tomorrow/this week/this month? What do you want to have achieved by this time next year?

- **What are your specific day-to-day goals?** The goals 'to be successful' or 'go global' aren't precise enough. Write a list of your big goals to get them out of your system, then drill these down into a list of day-to-day actionable steps.

- **Who are your muses?** Who do you admire in business? Could you read a book about or by them? On a personal level, which of your friends or family members inspire you? What personality traits do you most admire and how could they help with your own goals?

- **Who else can help you with your goals?** Is there anyone in your career network? Ask as many people as possible in your chosen industry for advice. You never know what they might offer. Consider seeking a business mentor in the same industry whom you can go to for advice.

- **Who do you trust to give their opinion about your product?** Ask friends who you value and who maybe have special insight themselves (eg, they use the product).

# FOUR
# Nailing Your Brand

While deciding the colours and considering different styles for polish bottles, I was also thinking
about the branding for Safe 'N' Beautiful products.
I needed a name for the polish, a logo and a design
strategy. This was when I found myself working all
hours again, researching everything from scratch.

Brand building doesn't happen overnight. I had to consider what would attract customers to my product and
how my product would be identified and marketed in
shops. First, I had to make major decisions, like what
the product would be called. 'Safe-Nails' wasn't what
I wanted to call the polish. I kept coming up with silly,
childish names. I wanted something fun to reflect a
product for the children's market but nothing seemed
to feel right.

One evening, I was discussing ideas with my husband, Dimitris. 'Safe-Nails doesn't fit with a fun name,' I said. 'I can't think of anything.'

'How about Snails?' Dimitris suggested.

I stared at him like he was mad. Then I thought about it. All children love finding snails in the garden when they're growing up, and I could design a cute character around this idea. In keeping with the high-end beauty industry, too, Paris is often likened to the shape of a snail shell, with its twelve districts that spiral out from the centre of the city.

The name 'Snails' would certainly grab attention. Like always, I ran the idea past my girls and when they giggled with delight, I knew it was the one. What had seemed like a mad idea was actually a good one.

Interviewing the creative people you want to work with and viewing their previous work beforehand is essential to ensure that you have a good working relationship with the creative helping develop your brand. I got in touch with a Greek designer (who I found on Freelancer.com) and explained the idea. He completely understood what I was trying to achieve.

# What makes a successful brand?

I didn't then know what a brand strategy was, but I soon learned it involves a deep understanding of your target audience, your brand message and 'voice'.

Brand has to be consistent. You need the same logo across your website, product, literature and stationery, and to use the same font and designs. A graphic designer or illustrator can help with this.

Your brand should appeal not only to your market but to their *emotions*. It should add value to someone's life and attract the customer with a strong voice. Bearing all of this in mind, I wanted Snails to be colourful, fun, and full of joy.

Of course, I wanted children to love the brand, but I also needed parents to trust it, to see a safe, quality product. This influenced my choice of bottle, bottle top and colour scheme. The word 'safe' had to be highlighted so parents could easily spot the word while browsing the shelves.

I talked my designer through my ideas for an eye-catching logo of a snail. The first concept was where the 'S' looked like the snail's tail. The snail looked fun, like a cartoon character who could slither off the bottle to play with the child. We went on to give the snail a name. I invited input from customers on the Snails Facebook page and 'Mirabelle' won the vote.

## Catch the consumer's eye

From day one, I decided to make Tiffany blue the standard colour for our products to appeal to both sexes. This shade of blue denotes quality and depth. I had also spotted how other brands had all gone for pink and I wanted my brand to stand out on the shelves.

Next I chose a memorable design for my business cards. A business card is your first introduction to your shopfront, and the first thing someone might receive from you following a face-to-face chat. To stand out from the crowd, especially at networking events, don't go for the classic rectangular-shaped white card – it will get lost with all of the others. Choose an eye-catching shape or colour.

In the early days, we opted for cards in the shape of birds, which also promoted that we were on Twitter, our first attempt at social media marketing. Using a bird along with a snail certainly caught the eye of potential clients. But we changed it regularly to keep it updated and follow newer trends. I want Snails to continually look fresh and at the forefront of innovation.

I then needed to find a copywriter to help with the wording on all the products. I found a British copywriter called Neil and we worked together, starting newsletters too. He also did the content of the brochures, the labels and the writing on the back of bottles. Neil had a great sense of humour and didn't take himself too seriously, which is similar to my character and the values I wanted for Snails. We were doing important work to make a quality product, but kept a fun and light-hearted approach to it. Like all the best things in life, Neil's writing was simple, catchy and easy to recall.

Neil came up with the idea of little girls illustrated on our products saying, 'I have snails on my nails.' Once again, when I repeated this idea to my own children, their faces lit up. We were onto a winner.

## Nail your web domain

I cannot stress enough how important it is to buy the web domains you need at the very start. Once your brand name is decided, you will need a website with this name, or something that is the nearest version of it.

I learned my lesson the hard way, because I didn't do this for all countries. For example, I bought safe-nails .com, but not for China or Germany, and when I wanted them at a later date, they were not available.

Be wary that other people spot when a domain has been bought and then try and sell them back to companies in the future for a higher price. It pays to think ahead. Many domains only cost around fifteen euros each, so it's worth the investment to snap up the names you want for the future too.

# The importance of packaging

Packaging is everything! I make no apologies for shouting this bit. You could have the best product in the world, but if it's not in eye-catching and beautiful packaging, forget about sales. In fact, forget about a distributor choosing your product either. High-quality, tempting packaging is what they're looking for.

When browsing a shelf of cosmetics, what do you do? You either gravitate towards the brands you already know and love, or you look at what new item catches your eye. If you see that the packaging is good quality, then you safely assume the product inside will be.

The packaging is the equivalent to a shopfront. It is the first introduction a consumer has with your product. It communicates what your product is all about.

Ideally, the packaging of a product should:

- **Be a thing of beauty.** Packaging should appeal to customers aesthetically and make them want to open it – or at least possess it.

- **Create an emotional response.** People should either admire it or feel compelled to need it in their lives. The old saying, 'If it's not beautiful or useful, throw it out' comes into play here.

- **Be sustainable.** Consumers are more savvy than ever about environmental issues and their own carbon footprint. We all feel better when we know the product we're buying doesn't harm our planet.

- **Stand out from the competition.** Don't copy your packaging. Don't blend into the crowd. Jump off the shelf instead!

- **Appeal to the five senses.** This will create a truly memorable brand experience. Sensory interactions with products boost sales and build loyalty. Sight, sound, feel, smell and taste – try to appeal to all of the senses wherever possible.

Snails had a strong identity with our use of colour, the snail character and high-quality packaging and polish. A parent picking up a shade would appreciate the sustainable bottle and promise of a safe product and a child would not be able to wait to play with it. Win–win!

While finalising our branding, I went to the LUXE PACK exhibition in Monaco, which showcases all the latest designs and trends, to get ideas and make sure our packaging stood up well alongside our competitors. I remember being at a booth looking at two ladies with Bulgari on their badges and thinking, 'Wow, there are some incredibly successful people here!' I was looking to put the finishing touches to my bottles. I knew something was missing from the design but I couldn't put my finger on it. Then we passed a booth selling ribbons, and I saw a little bow. I stopped and stared for almost half an hour at the booth not knowing why. Dimitris was patiently standing next to me.

I turned to him and said, 'Our bottles need a bow around the neck of each one. It can become our recognisable product feature.'

I ordered thousands of bows. I knew they would appeal to my little customers, and when I showed my daughters, my hunch was right, especially when they realised the bows could fit around their fingers like a ring. They loved them!

By then, I had also chosen my bottles. To begin with, I bought them directly from Italy, again choosing a high-quality product. When we returned to Greece, we spent hours carefully sticking the bows around the bottles ourselves. I had to ask a few friends to join in and help because I needed the bottles to be ready in time for an expo in London.

Then came our next big challenge: to sell Snails to the world.

## CASE STUDY: PATRICIA MONNEY, AVIELA SKINCARE

Patricia Monney set up her own business, Aviela Skincare, to make high-grade shea butter products. She was inspired by her daughter who had suffered an ankle injury and used shea butter massaged into her joints to help her walk again. This is Patricia's story:

Having no previous experience in cosmetics, it was a steep learning curve entering this industry! I returned to my childhood home in the northern region of Ghana to source the highest-grade shea butter nuts at the beginning. I wanted to help support the local economy, so I set up a women's co-operative, who sourced and prepared the fallen shea butter nuts. The nuts were then processed in the UK and made into the product.

At first, we sold Aviela Skincare in London stores that sold African products. But as sales grew and our product became more noticed, we were approached by higher-end distributors and I was advised to change our packaging to appeal to a wider customer base.

Our initial brand identity involved simple designs and simple packaging, which I designed myself. This reflected how natural our product is. Then the global retailer Whole Foods asked us to sell in their stores. This was a huge opportunity, and to my amazement, we sold out within two weeks. But then we were asked to reconsider our branding. We needed to take our brand identity to the next level and make it more appealing to the premium market. After all, what we had created was a premium product! Our feedback was that the current packaging did not quite reflect this.

This time, I employed a marketing consultant to do some research, which took a year or so. We also conducted a customer focus group and the feedback was so interesting. People told us there was nothing on the packaging which told the customer we were using a women's co-operative and this is something that would attract customers to buy it. So we rebranded, using higher-quality packaging and added a logo for the female co-operative. Our branding now reflects the quality of our product and we're in negotiation with high-end retailers to stock the product long term.

We have exciting times ahead of us. Being open to the idea of change and improving our brand has resulted in growth and success beyond anything we expected.

---

## TOP TIPS FOR NAILING YOUR BRAND

- Your brand needs to stand out in the crowd, so think of something that will be memorable for customers.
- Your brand design and message should be consistent. A designer can help you maintain consistency across your channels to help with this.

- Shore up the fundamentals – trademark your brand and products and secure any web domains you think you will want, even if that seems far off in the future.
- Take time to develop the perfect packaging. It's the shopfront to your brand when it's out in the world.

---

# FIVE

# Confronting The Challenges

You have made decisions about your brand. You have taken steps to have the product made. Now what? Well, this is often when the challenges will crop up, endlessly! Mistakes are unavoidable, so don't be afraid of making them. It's impossible not to make them when you're learning on the job. For me, this was like a crash course in business and finance, and I was not only the pupil but my own teacher too. Accept the fact that mistakes are part of growing a successful business and when they happen, learn from them and move on quickly.

One of my first major mistakes happened over my choice of bottles. I knew I wanted something high quality but didn't know where to find that. I had found a place in Greece but because they sold through a third party, their bottles were more expensive. I didn't realise the price was much higher than it would have been if I had gone direct, and it took me months to understand this. I was looking for something solid and aesthetically pleasing, and so I eventually found a place in Italy, a country famous for glass products.

The next challenge was to find a factory to fill the bottles. The factory in Paris didn't provide this service, which was also a shock to me. How was I going to fill thousands of bottles myself? I had visions of hand-pouring nail polish into fiddly bottles in my kitchen using a funnel. Then I realised I had to find a separate factory in Greece to do it, and of course this cost more money.

Whenever I thought I had finally got everything sorted, more challenges came thick and fast. I had all the enthusiasm, the brand ideas and had chosen the nail varnish and bottles, but I knew nothing about the business side of things. For example, the man who sent the bottles warned me that I needed the CE symbol on them.

'What is a CE symbol?' I asked.

He let out a familiar small sigh, then explained that CE stands for *Conformité Européenne*, the French for European Conformity. The CE mark means that the manufacturer takes responsibility for the compliance of a product with all applicable European health, safety, performance and environmental requirements.

I felt sick. I had no idea this was necessary. I was embarrassed at my ignorance, but I quickly shook this off. 'You are still learning,' I told myself. How could I expect to know everything when I had never done this before?

# Trademark your logo

When I had settled on the final logo for Snails, I trademarked Snails and Safe-Nails. I had not thought about trademarking until my bottle maker asked me if I had seen a lawyer to trademark my brand name. 'Otherwise you will see thousands of products called Snails if it's a success,' he warned me.

I felt suddenly overwhelmed but once again smiled and asked politely if he could help point me in the right direction to sort the issues out.

It's always best to do this first in your own country and then in your continent. If you have the budget, trademark internationally too (eg, the USA and China, if you are based in Europe).

It might have seemed premature for me to be thinking of expanding into such huge international markets, but why not? I hoped Snails would achieve global success and made all my decisions from the outset to ensure it would.

A local solicitor can help you with trademarking. There is no need to spend extra money on expensive lawyers – it's a simple enough request to make.

## Understand your process, then get going

The French factory owner told me I needed to find a chemist to help with the CE certificate and a lawyer for the trademark. I was grateful to him but was panicking inside. Everyone is different when stress hits their life and for me, my process is to freak out. I tend to think it's a catastrophe, cry, rant, release whatever I need to release for twenty-four hours. The next day, a calmness descends and I can get on with the job.

Different people will have different processes. You might need a week or a few hours. You might get angry or need to go for a run or even bang your head against the table. You might feel completely frustrated or wonder why you ever began trying this crazy idea. You might even want to give up.

It doesn't matter how you handle it. What matters is how you dust yourself off to try again. Now is the time to reignite your self-belief on a regular basis, because you'll need it.

It's important to take time out to do this. Inspirational books were a godsend to me during this start-up phase. I chose titles that helped me feel positive, grounded and mindful. I wanted to read about other people overcoming challenges so I could emulate them, and I still do this today. More recent titles I have enjoyed include Sophia Amoruso's #*GIRLBOSS*, and *How to Be an Overnight Success* by Maria Hatzistefanis.[9] All the books had one major message: one of hope. This was the feeling I had to focus on to make Snails work.

With a clearer head, I spoke to a chemist in Greece who helped me with the CE certificate. I needed to fill in forms for each country I hoped to export to. Every country has its own authorised company that registers bar codes for products, and every product needed its own barcode.

The Greek chemist was paid to test all the ingredients, then fill in the form for the Cosmetic Products Notification Portal (CPNP) and apply on my behalf. The portal registered the product officially to show its adherence to European regulations.

I asked her to explain the process so I could do it myself in the future. It's my personal preference to understand the ins and the outs of every part of my business. It makes spotting mistakes easier and allows me to build

---

9.  M Hatzistefanis, *How to Be an Overnight Success: Making it in business* (Ebury Press, 2017)

my knowledge. Even if I delegate jobs, I want to know how to do them.

Finally, after a few weeks, samples of my washable formula in the colours I had chosen were sent to my home to test. I have never been so excited to open a box!

With my daughters and husband by my side, we all watched as I took a deep breath, unscrewed the first ever bottle of Snails and painted my nails for the first time. Admiring the shiny colour on my fingernails, I could see this was a quality product. Then I reached for a tap to wash it off. The polish had glided on and washed off just as easily.

'I love it!' I cried.

Next, I tried it on my daughters' nails and even my husband Dimitris'. We all loved it, especially how easily it came off. We happily approved the product for the factory to carry on making more.

'One day, you will be happy the property business went bankrupt and Safe 'N' Beautiful was born,' I announced to my husband. He looked a bit shocked, but I had never been so sure of anything in my life.

But later, when I showed my friends, they were cynical.

'Why would someone want a nail varnish that just comes off?' one asked, holding the bottle up to the light.

I could see she was sceptical, but I didn't allow my disappointment to show. At the time, my friends didn't have children. I thought maybe once they did, they would understand. And that is exactly what happened.

Once we had decided the colours, I needed them to have names. So who did I ask? My daughters, of course. Here is the list:

- Raspberry pie
- Disco girl
- Candy floss
- Fairytale
- Make-a-wish
- Lollipop
- Bedtime stories
- Go Green!
- Secret diary
- Purple comet
- Mrs Carrot head
- Breathe easy (for the top coat)

The names were adorable and straight from a little girl's mouth, so I knew they would be relatable. From then on, I always asked for my daughters' opinion to 'baptise' the products. Children know best!

When I was finally happy with the product, I took a deep breath and made the initial order of twenty-five kilograms of each shade.

The bulks would last two years before they expired. The clock was now ticking to make this business a success.

## Trial and error

Finally, after overcoming the hurdles of making the products, I had to face the challenge of finding a distributor. Although I had set up an online shop, I knew the way to high volumes of sales was to sell into major stores, and I needed distributors across the world to do this. International trade fairs and expos are held every year for businesses to introduce their products to global distributors, and that's where I headed.

In January 2012, I arranged for Safe 'N' Beautiful to be introduced to the world at the London exhibition centre. I hoped we would find global distribution companies there or at least make lots of contacts who could help us. I dreamed of potential clients crowding around our products, eager to sell them on our behalf.

I had to pay £4,000 just to attend and I couldn't stretch my budget to afford a booth, so my husband and I made one by providing images to the organisers. I was unable to afford real child models, so I organised a photoshoot with my daughters and several of their friends. My copywriter had the idea of adding in four speech bubbles above the children's heads, saying phrases such as: 'Splish splash', 'Snails washes off', and 'I want Snails on my nails.' This visually conveyed the sense of humour and fun around our brand, and not only that, but it looked like it was designed by kids themselves. We also highlighted the fact the product was made in France and I was a mother who had developed it for her own children.

We finished off the booth with a grass carpet and Dimitris used his contacts in the building trade to have it transported over. Excited at the prospect of attracting attention for Snails for the first time, I also paid for a PR lady to travel from the north of England and stay in London to help promote my product.

But when I arrived, I found myself standing alone. Everywhere around me, people were chatting excitedly, but nobody spoke to me or took much notice of my booth. This was hardly the introduction of Snails to the world I'd hoped it would be.

After a few hours, I realised my mistake. This expo was aimed at people like manicurists and nail salon owners, not actual distributors. I left without any deals or speaking to anyone who could help. It meant the PR lady had nothing to work with either, so I paid for her services for nothing.

This was soul destroying, especially because I had spent so much on flights, hotels and pointless PR. Worse still, I had paid for another expo in Dubai the following month! This time I had paid for a pre-made booth so it was even more expensive. After paying for the production costs of my products, I was down to my last few thousand dollars. If the Dubai expo was a disaster too, I would have no money left to try and find a distributor.

My biggest failure was not understanding my market very well. Do your research before paying to attend events. Will you be able to book appointments to meet or network with people beforehand? Ideally, find someone to give you advice who has attended them before.

## When the going gets tough

There will be times when you feel like the world is against you, when nothing goes your way over and over again. This happened to us at the Dubai expo too. Already, this was a trip that could make or break Safe 'N' Beautiful. The stakes were so high, the stress was unbearable. I *had* to find a distributor, or I would go broke.

Once again, we had supplied images of our self-designed booth and I was thrilled with what we had planned, but we couldn't afford to have someone build it for us so had to build it ourselves. We took two friends along to help us out.

Everything was organised, or so I thought. Until I realised the building materials for our booth hadn't turn up! Time ticked on and by midnight, we were still waiting. The booth needed to be ready by 7am, when the doors opened to potential clients.

I thought my company was finished before it had got started. I had spent all my money and still wouldn't even have a distribution deal. I sunk to the floor in tears, thinking, 'This is the end. I might as well go home.' I couldn't believe how awful this situation was.

Luckily, some kind people at the expo managed to find our missing booth pieces and helped us put it together. Once again, it's other people you need to lean on at times to get over that finish line. I've always found being honest works to your advantage too. People like to help people, especially when things are hard. But even during this upsetting episode, I tried to keep things upbeat.

We finished building the booth at 3am and then fell into a hotel bed, exhausted. I got up after about an hour dozing, wired and unable to sleep, knowing today, something had to work out.

In the morning light, I was proud of what we had achieved. Our products on display looked very professional and with our two friends joining us to unpack the boxes and offer potential samples, it looked like Snails already had four employees. I kept my positive façade going all day, speaking to customers as they walked past. Then one of them stopped, listened and looked impressed.

Although I was honest and told him we were a start-up company, I didn't tell him we didn't have any distributors. Instead, I focused on the fact our product was made in a high-quality factory in France, knowing that France is recognised as a trusted cosmetics manufacturer. In fact, I had made sure we included a picture of the Eiffel Tower with a sign saying we were made in France. I also emphasised that I was a mum who had developed this product and had included the fact I was the owner of the business and a mother in my literature about the company.

Over the years, many successful children's products have been made by parents for other parents. The phenomenally successful Trunki, the suitcase for kids that can be sat on and pulled along, was an idea born by a dad who wanted to make travelling with children more fun. Parents are good at recognising problems and solving them. Distributors realise this too. Being a mother was an extremely useful selling point for my product and was one I was keen to capitalise on.

## Have fun with your product

The quality of a product sells, but so does the person selling it. Nobody will buy from someone who looks disinterested or lacks enthusiasm for what they're selling. Not only should you know everything about your product but you should also communicate your love for it.

Even today, I have lost none of my initial enthusiasm for Snails. At my expos, I always crack jokes, offer to paint the nails of everyone walking past – whether they're a suited-and-booted CEO or a young daughter of a visitor – and sometimes we even put music on and dance.

At the Dubai expo, I was nervous and anxious about not selling any of my products but when people did approach us, I made sure I was as welcoming as possible. I smiled, answered all their questions, offered samples and behaved like we were already a huge success. After all, I told myself, it was only a matter of time.

After an in-depth conversation with a distributor from Qatar, to my absolute shock, he placed one order of 10,000 euros worth of product there and then. I had my first big sale!

I could have jumped with joy but remained calm and professional, holding back my fists that wanted to punch the air. Luckily, he never asked us how many other clients we had or where else we sold the product. He might have been put off if he had known he was our first major sale.

By the end of this expo, I had sealed deals with distributors from Dubai, Saudi Arabia and, of course, Qatar.

Snails was in business.

---

### CASE STUDY: SALLY DEAR, DUCKY ZEBRA

Sally Dear is the founder of an ethical unisex children's clothing company called Ducky Zebra, which launched in 2021. The challenges she faced thanks to starting a business during lockdown were many. This is her story:

It's hard to avoid the fact that Ducky Zebra launched during a global pandemic – and without a shadow of a doubt, this has been our biggest challenge.

We were working on designs and samples while juggling lockdown life and home-schooling, managing significant production delays due to factory lockdowns, navigating photoshoots during the rule of six and dealing with shipping delays due to the Covid transport backlog.

We couldn't change the circumstances, so we had to accept them instead. We let go of our original timings and diverted our energy and attention to things we could control, such as building brand awareness and engagement. We tried to flip each hurdle into a positive. And we're a better brand because of it.

How? Well, we completely overhauled our designs during the first lockdown, focusing on the simple things we could still enjoy with our families, such as riding a bike or splashing in a puddle. The end result is a fantastic collection of fun clothes that children can relate to. To reduce the risk of mixing 'bubbles', we decided to photograph our own kids with their school friends, resulting in a natural, fun photoshoot full of laughter and excitement. It encapsulated our brand values of kindness and confidence perfectly without looking forced or staged.

Finally, the delays, while frustrating at the time, allowed us to build meaningful connections with like-minded businesses, write articles for magazines, build our social media following and create a sense of excitement around our launch that we couldn't have achieved with our original timings. Making the most of the additional time and viewing it as a positive has definitely helped us to overcome many of the pandemic challenges that have been thrown our way.

---

## TOP TIPS TO CONFRONT THE CHALLENGES

- When things go wrong, put on a brave face and the confident façade will eventually pay off.
- Again, shore up the fundamentals – trademark your brand and products.
- Hold out for that big break. If you have worked hard and done your research, have faith that it will come good.

- You only need a few distributors to believe in your product to get sales going. Choose them wisely and make sure they are people who truly believe in your product.

- Write down your biggest dreams and goals and refer back to these again and again. In the midst of confronting challenges, the overall goal is all too easy to forget, so keep reminding yourself of where you are going and why.

---

# SIX
# Price And Promotion

You can have made the best product in the world, but unless you find an efficient and committed distribution network, people won't know where to buy it. There is such fierce competition to place cosmetics in shops, it's hard to believe it's possible at first. But remember the idea for Snails came from watching my daughters play at home, and now it's sold in seventy-nine countries around the world. If there is a place for my product in shops around the globe, there is for yours too.

Once again, I did my research to prepare and came across the importance of the four Ps:

- Product
- Price

- Place

- Promotion

These key elements all affect one another. Not only did I need to get my product and price right, I had to find the right store that would promote it properly. For this, I needed to find the right distributors to make Snails a success.

But before we get into more detail on that, let's take a quick look at the finances, as these will help you determine the all-important price point for your product.

## Financing your product

I financed my business with savings at the beginning. But there are many options to consider. They include:

- Short-term loans

- Bank loans

- Crowdfunding

- Loans from family and friends

- Capital from investors

It is often the case that you begin by financing your dream one way and then need to secure a loan or investment to grow further. None of the options are without risks and I would only suggest getting a loan of any kind if you're convinced you can pay it off in full very quickly.

Later on, you could look for outside investment in your product. But in the early stages, this is unlikely to happen. Most investors only want to give money to tried-and-tested products. Even then, investment might not be for your business, because often it involves compromising your product for profits.

## Making it all add up

I knew nothing about profit margins or costs. But essentially you have to work out how much it costs to produce and promote your product, and factor this into the price.

First, I had to decide on what each bottle of nail polish would be priced at. I looked at how much a quality mid-range polish costs for sale in a pharmacy like Boots. Bottles began at three euros and went up to twenty euros for a bottle of Chanel polish. The American polish sold for ten euros, but that included custom fees.

I needed to work out the profit each party would make from each bottle too. The store ranged from 35% to 55% and of course, the distributor also wanted to make commission. At the end of the day, everyone wants to make a profit. All this information led me to decide a bottle of Snails should retail for eight euros a bottle.

## Finding the right distribution teams

At the same time as attending my first expo, I started an email campaign to find appropriate international distributors. I sent out hundreds of query emails to stores, shops and distributors themselves. This was a giant undertaking and I needed help.

I hired freelance researchers with experience in this field from the website Freelancer.com. I asked them to make me lists of all the stores and distributors who sold similar products for each European country and put this information into a spreadsheet.

I also hired translators to write the query letters explaining about our product. It was worth spending the extra cash on perfecting the language to make a professional-sounding enquiry. I sent off the letters to generic email addresses and crossed my fingers that people would get back to me. But of course, they didn't. It is vital that you find the personal email address of the store product buyers or distributors because people only reply to a personalised approach. Sending an email to an address beginning 'info@' almost never bears any fruit.

When I got a reply, I used Google Translate for the follow-up email, simply because I couldn't afford to spend money on translators for every correspondence. I used to say, 'Please forgive me for my poor French/Italian/German' (or whatever language it was), and most of the time the recipient thankfully did.

# Dealing with disappointment

Let me be honest. Despite taking time and effort to track down the right email addresses, the number of responses I got back was very disappointing. Out of thousands of emails, I only got a few replies, possibly as little as a 1% response rate.

This was a hard situation to deal with. I wasn't just being rejected, I was being completely stonewalled! Some days it felt like shouting into an empty cave, or feeling like a little person outside in the cold, waving at a window with successful people all warm inside, blanking me.

But I did not give up, and neither should you. I sent emails all over the world, even to places in the Baltics and Russia. I wasn't fazed by hard-to-reach markets, because at the time, I didn't know any better. And to my complete surprise, I received a reply from a Russian distributor. Sometimes it's the people you least expect to hear back from who contact you.

Russia is a hard market to crack. But I had done my research, responded to emails in Russian using Google Translate and incredibly, an enthusiastic young woman fell in love with the idea of Snails and began to sell it to stores all over Russia and Siberia.

# Creating a newsletter

Once you have compiled a database of email addresses, sending out a regularly updated newsletter keeps potential customers in the loop. I sent out our first around Christmas of 2011, emphasising how unique our washable nail polish was and that it was free from US custom fees.

There are many good reasons to send out a newsletter. It's an easy win. It can create a communication channel you didn't expect, puts your product at the forefront of a buyer's mind, and can increase traffic to your website.

Again, it's worth taking your time and employing others' expertise to make sure it looks professional. Using eye-catching graphics, revealing the latest news and making it quick and easy to read is key. You don't want to overload the reader with information – it should be short, snappy and create a sense of intrigue. You will only have seconds to persuade them to keep on reading.

Keep in mind it's a case of quality over quantity too. You don't want to spam people's email accounts. You want to inform them rather than annoy them.

Two recommended pieces of software for the email newsletter include services called Constant Contact and MailChimp. They have analytics software to let you know how successful the newsletter campaign is, who is reading and responding to your communication.

## Sending samples

If someone replies, they will often want to know more, and fast. A press pack at the ready is vital to give them all the information they need. But nothing sells quite like a sample of your brilliant product.

I made the decision early on to always treat potential customers like VIPs, so I didn't send small samples. I sent them the real full-sized products. Nor did I charge for samples. At times, when I visited factories making bottles, I was asked to pay for a sample and I always declined. It sends out the wrong message to a client. You are persuading them to fall in love with your product, not feel grateful to be allowed a proper look at it. So I put together a glossy sales kit on high-quality paper with a full-sized bottle of Snails for them to enjoy.

After many weeks and months of sending out emails and sample kits, people began to take an interest. From my query letters and sample packs, I found more distributors in France and Germany. After months of trying to sell Snails, I had over ten distributors.

The dream was coming true.

# Putting your product in good hands

Although I was thrilled to have any interest in Snails, I also wanted to ensure my business was in good hands. I asked about the distributors' credentials, their experience and, importantly, why they liked Snails and how they saw it being marketed. I always considered people's enthusiasm more important than experience. I have never forgotten that dismissive phone call with the American nail polish distributor, and vowed never to treat anyone in such a manner. It is true that enthusiasm can make up for lack of experience.

I also carried on being flexible with my minimum orders. I believed my product would prove itself quickly and fly off the shelves, so clients could always come back for more. At the end of every conversation, I had a heart to heart with every distributor personally. I said to them, 'Safe 'N' Beautiful is my baby, something I have built and nurtured myself. Please take care of my company like you would your own baby, and nurture the product so it grows. You are responsible for the appearance of Snails in stores and for what is written in the media, and I believe you will do an excellent job.'

Most people responded well to the personal approach. If you make it clear that you're trusting someone to do a brilliant job for you, they will want to fulfil the expectation.

This is not to say things always worked out. Sometimes sales were poor at six-monthly reviews. At this point, I would ask for a meeting with the distributor and see why things went wrong. More often than not, it was external factors, such as their country's economy, local issues with importing, or the legislation authority changing their rules.

Occasionally there were no such extenuating factors and I would be honest and query their sales techniques, and we'd sit down and see what could be changed with the marketing. But this was a rare event. Overall, I was lucky enough to find an incredible network of people who genuinely loved S'N'B's products and wanted to see Snails succeed.

# Brand endorsement and celebrities

There is nothing like a celebrity endorsing a product as a way to boost sales. Sales can skyrocket within hours of a celebrity promotion and it's a powerful way to secure free marketing.

It's every cosmetic company's dream to get a free endorsement for their product, especially if it's not a paid advert, because customers will assume the celebrity must really like it.

But I had to be realistic. I doubted any A-lister would want to advertise Snails for free and I was too shy to contact any British celebrities, but I did think of one famous Greek actress who might somehow help. There are only a few internationally famous Greek people in the world and as a Greek lady promoting an unusual product for my country, I decided to take a chance. I contacted the actress Nia Vardalos, who starred in *My Big Fat Greek Wedding,* via a direct message on Twitter.

When you're cold calling anyone, it's always advisable to find a common link, so I explained that I was also Greek and had just built my own company. Then I offered to send samples to Nia's young daughter. Nia replied, telling me she would tweet about the product and wished me good luck. I was over the moon and saw sales go up via the website straight away.

Nia was the only celebrity I managed to contact, but it was worth the effort.

In a funny twist, the Russian distributor managed to get Snails featured in *Vogue* magazine, and by mistake, a photo of Tom Cruise and his daughter Suri was placed within the piece. Readers assumed Suri had used Snails, so our sales shot up.

Early on, I also pretended to be my own PR lady, firing off emails to bloggers after researching them myself. I had so much to learn, such as which blogger was more influential than others, what they reviewed, what sort of products they liked. It took hours and hours of intensive research. Today, Instagram is the place to find influencers for businesses, but back in 2011, researching the biggest bloggers and emailing them directly was the best way forward.

Once I had worked out which bloggers reviewed products like mine, I sent them my free full-sized samples. Many of them gave us good reviews, commenting favourably about how smoothly the nail polish went on, how they loved the fun packaging and, if they had a daughter, how much she loved it. As a result of these kind comments, I saw sales go up via the website.

---

### CASE STUDY: HELEN KING, BLUE EYES BOW TIES

Helen King loved sewing and decided to start a small bow tie making business, Blue Eyes Bow Ties. This is her story:

I set up Blue Eyes Bow Ties in late 2016 because I longed to leave my all-consuming job as a history teacher. I thought about what product I could make, sell without people needing to try on, then post, and bow ties came to mind. I chose fabrics I loved and made them all by hand.

I first sold them on eBay and they did well, so I made a website and set up a Shopify account. Then one day I got an email from someone in the wardrobe department for the BBC. They ordered three bow ties. I contacted them to ask for more details but they asked me not to put anything on social media.

Nearly a year later, they got in touch to say the black-and-gold bow tie was going to be worn by Jodie Whittaker, the actor who plays Doctor Who.

The bow tie was worn in the series trailer. I was so excited, I couldn't believe it.

This time, I was allowed to put the news on my website and I posted a photo of Doctor Who wearing the bow tie. The SEO picked up the link and soon I had fans of the TV series all over the world putting in an order. I was working day and night to keep up with the demand and it really helped my small business to fly.

Afterwards, I was interviewed by local TV and radio about my product, which led to further sales. I had no idea how powerful a celebrity featuring a product could be, even if they are a fictional character who is out of this world.

---

### QUESTIONS TO CONSIDER WHEN PRICING AND PROMOTING YOUR PRODUCT

- What are your profit margins? What does it cost you to produce and promote your product? What cut is your distributor or retailer entitled to?
- What are competitors' products priced at?
- Who specifically do you need to reach to get your product out there on shelves? Can you hire a freelancer to help you identify them and/or communicate with them?
- What can you do to increase awareness of your product? Can you send samples? Can you create a newsletter?
- Are there any celebrities or influencers who can endorse your product to boost sales?

---

# SEVEN
# Keeping Up With Demand

To my surprise, it was easy for us to enter the nail polish market via the Dubai expo, and after finding more distributors via the email newsletter campaign, I suddenly had a product to deliver. I couldn't wait to get back to Greece to get started. So much was at stake.

My next challenge was to deal with the admin for sales. There were so many things I was still learning. For example, to send products to an Arabic country, a Greek registered business needs to be a member of the Arab–Hellenic Chamber of Commerce. I had to attend the Qatar Embassy to get the appropriate paperwork and stamps. Different countries required different certificates, so this was a time-consuming process visiting the different embassies.

Next, we had to send a contract to the distributors. I had no idea how to do this, so who did I turn to? Yes, Google again! I read up about the contracts and the importance of making them work in the favour of the business, such as reassuring the distributor that they would be given exclusive rights to sell the product, but in return, the distributor should be required to order a minimum number and do some marketing on the business's behalf, eg, taking the product to an expo, or advertising it on TV or in a magazine.

I found a lawyer to draw me up a template contract. I adjusted it for Safe 'N' Beautiful's needs and then I sent it out. I had to negotiate in the early days, but was flexible and accommodating of distributors' demands. For example, if they didn't want to advertise on TV but would do so in magazines, I allowed this. At first, I used my solicitor to handle the negotiations, but soon felt confident to manage it myself, especially as most distributor negotiators spoke English.

## Be open-minded about every sale

In the beginning, I wasn't fussy who I sold to. If it was a company, big or small, I took every order gratefully. I still felt like an amateur, working from my kitchen table and making calls from the house phone. But I didn't dwell on my lack of experience. The fact was, I was taking orders and people wanted my product. The rest could be learned along the way.

Until you are established, keep an open mind regarding new clients. I have seen other businesses fail due to being snobby or fussy about initial clients or distributors. One friend set up a business in Greece. He had made an incredible product, paying so much attention to the quality, the brand and design. I was very impressed. But within a year, his business had gone bust. This was because he insisted on a fixed minimum order quantity. This was unsustainable, sadly. You cannot be picky when you are new to a market, whatever that market is.

I picked up ways of securing sales when people wanted to ask questions. I was always positive, personable and light-hearted, but I also listened more than I talked. People want to do business with approachable and flexible people, not precious sales people with unrealistic goals. Remember, you're not only selling your product, you're also selling yourself as a person to do business with.

## Pretend to be bigger than you are

Being new to the market is a major challenge for every start-up company. No distributor wants to be a company's first distributor, ie, the guinea pig or experiment. And nobody in the business wants to admit they have no experience.

Would the distributors have bought Snails from my little booth in Dubai if they had realised I knew nothing about exporting and had no clients yet? Probably not. But we all have to start somewhere. We all need someone to give us our big break.

I had to act as if my business was more successful than it was at the start. I never misled anyone, but I created the impression I had other employees before I could afford them. In the early days, on the rare occasion when people replied to my emails, I always replied via the info@safe-nails.com email address rather than my personal one. I wanted to give the impression that I had an assistant working for me. I even answered the phone sometimes putting on a different voice and then 'transferred' the call to Jeanette, while I tried not to giggle.

To improve the emails I fired off, I asked my English friend, Michelle, who had better English-speaking skills than I did to pitch in and help. In her spare time, she logged into the email and replied in perfect English. She did a better job with initial communication and I could afford to employ her for a few hours a week. Suddenly I had my first employee, and I wasn't doing it alone for real. I couldn't have thanked her enough.

# Patience is key

Being patient and diligent in the early days is key to building opportunities. Nobody can become a success overnight. It's easy to get caught up in the excitement and expect things to fall into place immediately once you have secured those first major deals. But this is the time to pay attention to detail.

Although securing the Middle Eastern distributors was a turning point, they didn't suddenly make Snails a success. I had much further to go. For many years, I had a series of small but dedicated distributors. I learned a lot from them. I spoke to them often, checked their progress and tried to understand their markets. One thing I did learn was what other cultures were looking for with nail products. I spoke to a few Muslim women who told me they had to pray five times a day and were not allowed to wear nail polish while doing so. A couple of them asked me, 'Do you sell washable nail polish for adults?' I admitted I didn't, but filed this idea in my mind for later on.

The next break came with the German market. The distributor there secured sales through Amazon. I had tried to open an Amazon account for Safe 'N' Beautiful in the early days, but it wasn't a huge success. It's a complicated process and not as easy as it looks. Not only do you need the correct bar codes, but you also need to make sure you include keywords that link up with similar products, otherwise customers can never find your shop. For an amateur, it's a tricky system to navigate.

Thankfully, the German distributor knew what she was doing and sales had a bounce.

## Slow like a snail

By the end of 2012, our first year, we had made the money back on our product and were a whopping 25,000 euros in profit. This, by small business standards, was a huge success. But growing too fast is as dangerous as no sales at all. There are several reasons for this, which even surprised me. They include:

- **Cash flow problems.** This often means you lose track of what is coming in and what is going out. I kept a spreadsheet with costs and sales, keeping a close eye on the numbers so that I wasn't overstretching myself.

- **Not adapting along the way.** Suddenly when you have more sales, you need to keep up with demand, and this means hiring staff, moving to bigger premises and paying out a lot more. This is a fine balancing act. Choosing to expand too fast can lead to it all crashing down if you don't have everything in place first or if you cannot keep up with the growth.

- **You lose sight of the quality and the brand.** If you're struggling to keep up with demands and don't have the infrastructure to keep on top of it, standards will slip. For example, I couldn't bottle my product myself yet, so had to keep orders manageable. If I had tried to do it myself at the kitchen sink with a funnel, the quality would certainly have gone down. I wanted to make the distribution networks I was establishing a success before we continued our growth.

# Our biggest challenge

Let's rewind a little bit, to the time after the sales were ordered and the products were ready for delivery, when I came up against my biggest hurdle yet. This was the moment I had to deal with the horror of exporting products from Greece and the unbelievable amount of excess paperwork that went with this. Exporting from Greece was an absolute minefield and there was no support helpline for small businesses.

I had to find an accountant who could help with the paperwork, as it was impossible for me to do. But because it was still rare for Greek companies to export products, I couldn't find any accountants who could help with this niche requirement. My accountant had to ask others to help him.

I also spent hours on the phone asking for assistance from the authorities about what paperwork I needed to fill in and nobody was available. Incredibly, there was no department set up for this. This was a tiring and frustrating time but I kept going. I had to find a way myself. Luckily, the distributors didn't appear to notice any delays, and I hid the difficulties.

I've always found that even when you reach crisis point, maintaining a polite and calm façade at all times, despite what's going on behind the scenes, is best. Nobody needs to know you're having a bad day or how frustrating you're finding the process. They just want your quality product to sell.

## Snails growing bigger

Once I had overcome the exporting issue, to keep up with our sales demands it was time for Safe 'N' Beautiful to find a bigger home. By 2012, Snails had well and truly outgrown our kitchen worktop, so I rented our first office and storage space close to my home, in the business district of Athens. It was a small unit with a garage above to use as a warehouse. This reminded me of Essie Weingarten, who had also started with a garage for her nail business.

It was around this time that I was travelling back from a business trip to Germany when I spotted Snails on sale in a shop at the airport. When I saw the S'N'B sales stand by the till, with the familiar logo and graphics I had spent hours choosing, I drew a breath. This was a surreal moment, seeing Snails out in the wild for the first time. I couldn't quite believe it.

The lady behind the till saw my reaction and smiled. 'These Snails nail polishes sell very well. They're lovely, aren't they?'

I giggled and explained that I was the mum who had invented Snails. She looked at me like I was joking!

Back home, I excitedly told Dimitris. Once he had laughed at my idea of our household income being reliant on nail polish, but now he appreciated it was a thriving business and was proud of my achievement.

We had grown by now to such an extent that it was time to invite more people to join the Snails family and hire staff.

---

## CASE STUDY: ESTHER ROCHE, DEROISTE NATURAL BEAUTY

Esther Roche set up DeRoiste Natural Beauty to create natural organic, toxin-free products aimed at both adults and young people. Her products are designed to appeal to every person who loves looking after their skin, regardless of skin tone or gender. This is her story:

The inspiration behind my business was to create a wholly natural product that was suitable for the skin of both adults and kids. As a mum of many, I knew it was a product I'd like to see on the shelves. My initial challenge was how I was going to finance my start-up business, having been turned down for a start-up loan.

I discovered there are a huge number of resources available freely online. You don't need to do an expensive business course to find out the information you need to start a business. I found my local Chamber of Commerce and Local Enterprise Partnership groups really helpful.

My bank, NatWest, also offered free business courses, so I took one of those and then found out about a crowdfunding campaign via the NatWest Back Her Business scheme, which provided funding for successful campaigns. It was a challenge but I did manage to reach my target successfully, raising the funds within twenty-eight days which was the duration of the campaign. This meant I could afford to launch four products instead of two. Along with this, I was saving as much of my income as possible so I could put it towards other costs.

Another issue I faced was sourcing the packaging, due to the large minimum order quantities required. Fortunately for me, I was connected to a fellow mum who was able to help me work with smaller packaging manufacturers that had lower minimum order requirements.

After my launch, I managed to secure a place on a showcase for products in John Lewis, which was an enormous boost. It is a dream come true for my product to be sold there.

My main advice is to network and research online. You can find out everything you need to know about setting up a new business and there is no need to pay for the information that's already out there. Finally, always only take on any debt when your business is in the position to be able to pay it back quickly.

## TOP TIPS FOR EXPORTING YOUR PRODUCT SUCCESSFULLY

- Understand the exports/customs rules of your own country and the rules of the country you're selling into.

- Write down a strategy for each market. Different countries will require different things. Translate literature, review the tone and adapt communications to fit the target market culture if necessary.

- Once contracts with the distributor are in place, familiarise yourself with the cargo shipment process.

- Double-check the marketplace in each country you're selling to. Ask your distributors for local knowledge if needed. Having a distributor living in the country, able to speak the language and understanding the culture is essential here.

- Make sure your product quality meets that country's standards and regulations.

- Insure your business against late or no payments or negotiate upfront payments. Insure your goods too.

- Ask for help. At international trade events, you might be able to meet other friendly SMEs to give advice. This wasn't possible for me, but it's one of the reasons why I am writing this book. It might help others in Europe and the UK navigate the processes.

- Consider opening a multi-currency bank account to avoid overpaying on fees.

# EIGHT

# Learning To Be A Leader

If you begin a company, you will have to be prepared to lead it. To settle is to allow your company to look like every other company out there, and you want the opposite. You want to stand out.

But being a leader does not come naturally to all of us. Although I had a little experience working as a 'boss' for the kids' spa company and as an interior designer, I had no direct experience hiring full-time staff and managing a team.

While I was getting Snails off the ground, I kept Kids Spa Parties going, letting the manicurists who helped me with it continue running it for 50% of the profit. A few years later, I handed the whole business over to them because I needed to focus fully on Safe 'N' Beautiful.

It was time for me to become a boss.

## Hiring the right people

First, I advertised for staff in my local newspaper. I didn't know exactly what I was looking for, but I would trust my instincts when I found them.

It's common sense to want to choose the right people to work in your company. The costs of getting it wrong are huge financially and bad for morale. I wanted to find someone as enthusiastic as me about Snails, and someone with a hard work ethic. I don't think people necessarily need to have relevant experience – to me, the attitude and an ability to learn on the job is just as important. I still thought of the American distributor who had refused to allow me to sell her products in Greece. I wonder if she regrets that now!

My first employee was a woman called Sylvie Soulou, who is half French and half Greek. We instantly clicked during the interview, because I am also half Greek and half British, so we bonded over having joint nationalities. We shared a certain mentality where we don't feel we belong definitively to either culture.

Sylvie had no background in cosmetics but had worked in tourism. She was a great communicator and knew how to work with people from other cultures. It was a huge bonus that she spoke fluent French as that would help with our sales pitch. I liked her open, chatty and honest style.

I was completely upfront with her straight away and explained I couldn't afford a fat salary but I hoped the company might expand in time. She understood our brand and loved Snails from the moment she saw it. Her interest was genuine and infectious. Her job was to work with distributors and purchase all raw materials. Today, Sylvie still works for me as managing director and she is one of my closest friends.

The next member of our team was Lia Karpatseli, whom I employed to help with our packaging. She also had no experience working for a cosmetics company but loved the idea of Snails, being a mother herself. I was struck by her sunny nature too. She clearly took her role seriously and was eager to do every job well, and I never regretted giving her the role.

## Tips for hiring the staff you need

Having a prepared set of questions helped with the formal recruitment process, but after interviews, I had an informal chat too. I wanted to get to know people, notice what made them tick and listen carefully to their answers.

One question I asked was, 'What do you aspire to do?' The candidate's goals can reveal a lot about their motivations and abilities. Ideally you need someone who has enough ambition to want the company to do well, but also to be committed to the position they've applied for. One thing I always check is how many years a potential employee has worked at the previous jobs, to gauge their sense of loyalty and dedication.

Here are some other lessons I learned about hiring people:

- **Follow up on references.** I always made sure I asked for the candidate's latest reference. Even if people have gaps in their employment – and many people do in Greece – I needed to see they were able to show commitment to a job.

- **Realise experience isn't everything.** I wouldn't employ an inexperienced accountant, but there are many roles that can be taught, and intelligence and willingness to learn are as important as having done the job previously. I had no experience working in cosmetics beforehand, so why should I have demanded others did?

- **Consider the work culture you want to encourage.** I work closely with my team and the culture at work needs to be easy-going but hard-working. I wanted my staff to reflect the values I hold dear. I expect my staff to respect one another, whatever their position is in the company. Whether you clean the office or are the head manager, you have an important role to play.

- **Listen to how someone speaks in the interviews.** Someone who says 'I' or 'me' a lot might be self-obsessed. Listen to their anecdotes about working in a team. I am not looking for perfection, but I expect people to have a strong sense of community and team spirit.

## Letting go of control

Once I had distributors and an employed team in place, I had to let go of many of the jobs I juggled. After building my business from scratch, this was surprisingly challenging to do. I often wanted to step in and say, 'I'll do it', even if I didn't need to, or had hired someone perfectly capable of doing the job for me. It wasn't because I am a control freak – it's because I care and I had grown accustomed to being involved in every aspect of Snails. But my job as a leader is to manage overall, not to micromanage everything.

Leading a company comes in many forms. My company is still small because I like it being this way. We sell across so many countries, but I like the intimacy and family feel of our organisation. Other companies grow to the size where many other managers are necessary and this is when you might need to undertake a leadership course or develop your skills.

I had to learn to lead from the front and develop myself as part of the brand. Again, this was all new to me. I agreed to be interviewed many times by newspapers or media companies, including the DW channel. I was happy to share my personal story of being a mum who started a new business to help my family, so that I could inspire other women to forge ahead with their own dreams and ambitions.

I am not famous and my product is my brand. But I had to be aware of my image and the need to avoid negative publicity.

## Top tips for being a boss

The biggest leadership lessons I have learned as CEO include the need to keep the company growing and your team motivated. As you scale up, the role of CEO changes to creating big-picture strategies rather than performing day-to-day tasks. My job now is to think of how to build awareness of our brand as a whole.

Other lessons I've learned are:

- Have clear goals and expectations for your staff. From the start, make duties and roles very clear and what is the expected workload.

- Keep up staff morale. Encourage regular treats and time for staff to get together. If your team like one another, they will work better together as a team. If morale is high, good staff will want to stay long-term.

- Trust your team. Trust increases a sense of safety and openness. It means if things go wrong, people are more likely to speak up, and any issues involving orders or quality, for example, can be ironed out. A culture of trust creates a dynamic workplace where people feel able to make decisions quickly and effectively. A place that is full of trust is a pleasant place to work. Encourage your team to do more than they think they can do and encourage an innovative rather than a copycat culture. Problems are solved with creative solutions.

- Show compassion. This is in my nature, and even if I am the boss, I put my human side first. If you treat your staff well, they will have more respect for you and the company, and they'll want to do their best.

## Avoiding burnout

There is another reason for learning to delegate tasks in the day-to-day running of a busy thriving company: avoiding exhaustion.

In 2013, the uniqueness of Snails was validated when Ralph Lauren Europe came knocking to feature our product in their Milan show. I felt then that we had achieved many of our major goals. We had begun to sell our product all over the world and Snails was a sustainable, viable business. But the success came at a price I had never expected to pay.

At first, I started to have bad headaches when I stared at my computer screen. Then one day, when my husband came to the office late at night to ask when I was coming home, he saw my eyes were streaming.

'What is the matter?' he asked urgently. Worried for me, Dimitris took me to hospital, where they ran some tests. I also had a bad headache that hadn't shifted all day.

'You are suffering from stress caused by overwork,' the doctor declared. 'You're burnt out.'

I couldn't understand what he meant. I loved my work and had made Snails a success. Why should I stop?

But my body was telling me otherwise. I had been doing long days, up to sixteen hours, and since I started two years previously, I had spent thousands of hours concentrating in front of a screen.

This happened just two weeks before we were due to fly abroad for an expo. I knew I had to carry on, so I explained to the doctor that I couldn't give up now. 'I have important meetings to attend,' I said, fearful of missing anything.

'It's not about giving up,' the doctor replied. 'You will soon get to the point where you can't even press a button to call a nurse. So it's best to rest now before that happens.'

This warning shocked me. I had no idea how bad things had become.

I had to respect the boundary my body had given me. I immediately took a few days off, then only did the minimum of what was needed for a week or so until the headaches subsided. Really, I needed longer than this, but the expo trip was crucial.

What I did learn, however, was to ask for help. I asked two friends to come with us to the Middle East and asked Michelle to help with more emails. It felt strange delegating work, but needs must. This gave me the chance to see that I could also get more done when other people pitched in.

Later on, back at the computer at home, one of my daughters burst into the room. 'I hate Snails!' she cried.

I was shocked and looked up from my keyboard. 'Baby,' I asked gently, 'why do you say this?'

'Because Snails takes up all your time. You come home late and we don't see you so much,' she said.

This broke my heart. I was so upset. What had I done? All of my success felt like it was for nothing if my little daughters resented what I did for a living.

I am sharing this story because sadly it's a fact of life that 'having it all' is impossible, especially if you're starting a company and have a family. At least at first, you will need to be prepared to work long hours. Eventually you might not have to, but at the beginning, there will be sacrifices to make. It doesn't mean it's not worthwhile, especially if it becomes successful, but it's important to know the reality.

I held my daughter tightly in my arms and promised I would soon be able to take more time off. A few short years later, I was able to take the extra time off to spend with my family and choose my own hours. In a regular job for someone else, I'd never have had this choice, so it was all worthwhile in the end.

## Be mindful of your mind

This burnout episode taught me a valuable lesson: to look after my own body and mind when I am doing too much. This means taking regular screen breaks, eating healthily, and trying to switch off as much as possible. I also took up knitting. This is a mindful activity that forces me to be present in the moment. It empties my brain and relaxes my body.

Being a good businesswoman does not mean making yourself available 24/7. In fact, it is the opposite. You will become worn out and less effective at your job if you try to be there for everyone at all times. At one point, I kept my phone by my bed and when I got emails from America, I would immediately respond to them, even if I was half-asleep at 3am. But I have learned that things don't need an immediate response. People can wait, and I can delegate too.

Around this time, I began to extend my reading to other memoirs and inspirational books about examining the mind and finding a better pace in life. I realised too, that without relaxation, the sense of enjoyment and creativity is eroded. And I need to be creative to keep ideas for Snails fresh and inspiring.

One book I loved was *The Monk Who Sold His Ferrari* by Robin Sharma.[10] This book tells the story of Julian Mantle, a lawyer forced to confront the spiritual crisis of his out-of-balance life. After a heart attack, he decides to sell all his possessions and trek to India. On the life-changing trip, he meets Himalayan gurus who offer powerful, wise and practical lessons, teaching him to be present and to nurture the spiritual self rather than being obsessed with accruing material possessions.

I agree with this philosophy. We live a relatively simple life. I have never chased the dream of having a Ferrari – my car is ten years old! I also wear trainers to the office. The only materialistic things I want to spend my money on is my kids. I'd much rather use

---

10. R Sharma, *The Monk Who Sold His Ferrari* (Harper Thorsons, 2015)

my money to take them to Disneyland than have exotic holidays for myself.

I also enjoyed the Dalai Lama's book series *Be Inspired*, which includes the four books, *Be Happy, Be Here, Be Angry* and *Be Kind*. These take Buddhists' philosophies and compare them to real life.[11] I always felt a sense of compassion and calm reading his words, and I tried to see how I could incorporate his teachings into my own life. Everyone can keep growing from within. It's something that remains on my to-do list for life.

*Good Vibes, Good Life* by Vex King is also a brilliantly uplifting book. King is an Instagram guru who overcame adversity from his childhood to become a source of hope for young people. I loved King's wisdom about prioritising self-care and overcoming toxic energy, as well as confronting the inevitable challenges. These words really resonated with me: 'Step out of your comfort zone and face your fears. Growth takes place when you're challenged, not when you're comfortable.'[12]

Snails was all about taking my life in a new direction and stepping firmly out of my comfort zone of motherhood and the job I had previously had. I jumped into the unknown. I felt lost and panicked at times, but I kept moving past this and carried on sending emails,

11. T Gyatso, His Holiness the 14th Dalai Lama, *Be Inspired* (Hampton Roads Publishing Company, 2019)
12. V King, *Good Vibes, Good Life: How self-love is the key to unlocking your greatness* (Hay House UK, 2018)

thinking of ideas, researching and making notes, even when it seemed like the idea of a washable nail polish could only be a pipe dream.

King's words about changing your attitude to your situation, about taking control when you feel out of control, made sense to me too, not just in regard to building the business but also recovering from my burnout. As a woman and a mother, I have other needs and responsibilities, such as going for a coffee with my girlfriends, having a manicure, relaxing with my daughters. And that's OK.

Shifting your perception of rest is revolutionary in many ways. You have to give yourself permission to do it. But taking time for relaxation makes me a more energetic, creative businesswoman and therefore makes my business stronger and more successful. Resting well is just as important for your business as working hard.

---

## CASE STUDY: LEAH STEELE, SEARCHING FOR SERENITY

Leah Steele gave up her job as a lawyer after she suffered from a prolonged episode of burnout. Now she runs Searching for Serenity, a business coaching service for corporate people who suffer from burnout. She shares her expertise about burnout in the workplace here:

We should not see burnout as an inevitable side effect of working hard. Most of us cannot just stop and take a year-long sabbatical to recover. Even if we did, nothing would change when we returned to work without a recognition of what burnout is.

Burnout is systemic in our society and comes from our approach to work, our values, and even learned behaviour from parents. It means we've entered 'survival mode' and can be prevalent when we're trying something new or trying to climb the ladder quickly.

A recent Gallup poll said two-thirds of people in 2018 were suffering from burnout and this leaped to more than three quarters in 2020, after the pandemic hit.[13] But if we understand what burnout is, we can avoid it altogether.

When you're enjoying a job, it's harder to burn out, but when you're acting out of fear or pressure, then it's easy for it to creep up. There are five stages to workplace burnout:

1. **The honeymoon.** This is at the beginning, when you're fine, working hard and enjoying what you're doing.

2. **Initial challenges**. This is when you're realising the world might not work in your favour.

3. **The plateau.** Here, you might find yourself working harder and harder, repeating patterns or cycles as you try to overcome the challenges.

---

13. R Pendell, '7 Gallup Workplace Insights: What we learned in 2021', Workplace, 1 January 2022, www.gallup.com/workplace/358346 /gallup-workplace-insights-learned-2021.aspx, accessed 25 June 2022

4. **Acute crisis.** This is when you're working far longer and more intensely than your body can manage.

5. **Habitualised burnout.** This is chronic exhaustion.

Once we understand the build-up to burnout, we can learn how to avoid it. We can ask, before it's too late, 'Do I really need to deal with all the tasks myself? Can I ask for help, either from family, friends or employing someone?'

Just because you can do something, doesn't mean you should. Women often find it particularly challenging to stop and ask for help because they enjoy multitasking and are worried that if they can't manage alone, they'll feel like a failure. But burnout does not have to be normalised. We all deserve time to rest and recover.

---

## TOP TIPS FOR MAKING REST A PRIORITY

· Leave your phone outside your bedroom. Never wake up and look at it first thing in the morning or last thing at night.

· Leave weekends completely free for your own time. This might not be possible in the very early days of building the business, but when you can allocate at least one day a week to be completely work-free, do it!

· Learn what relaxes you. I have recently discovered a massage can relax me quickly. I also like to zone out in front of Netflix. Try new hobbies and find out what you like! Remind yourself that you deserve this time for you.

- Know rest is a vital part of being successful. Nobody can work 24/7, and no one should think of relaxation as a waste of time.

---

## NINE

# Developing Your Brand

A successful brand is distinctive, competitive, and visible to the target market. Once all this is established, it needs to be consistent, so customers can recognise it. At the top of your agenda should be keeping your brand on message – but what does that even mean?

You need to recognise what is popular about your brand and carry on doing the same things that people love. Consistency builds customers' loyalty. They gain confidence in your product, which inspires them to buy it repeatedly and makes your brand stand out among competitors.

I wanted S'N'B products to be high-quality, fun and accessible, appealing to both adults and kids, and this is what my customers liked too. Although I have never been bored by Snails, someone once told me that if you're doing the same thing over and over again successfully and feel jaded at times, then you're doing it right. For me, using the same colour palette, fonts, styles and messaging created brand recognition in my target market.

Safe 'N' Beautiful had become a global company and it was key to keep the brand on message but also appropriate for individual countries' cultures. I have regular catch-ups with my overseas distributors to make sure the brand is working for their markets.

## Communicating your brand

Since we started, we have marketed S'N'B products on Twitter, Facebook, email, and in national and regional press. One of the most efficient ways of communicating our message has always been via our newsletter to keep everyone updated about new products. But social media is a necessary part of your strategy. One survey by Statista showed that 96% of beauty brands have an Instagram account[14] and a Facebook survey reported that 74% of consumers on Instagram see a brand with an Instagram account as 'relevant', with 54% of regular

---

14. Statista Research Department, 'Share of brands that have an Instagram profile as of March 2016, by category', Statista, April 11 2016, www.statista.com/statistics/305292/worldwide-instagram -brand-adoption-rate-category, accessed 26 May 2022

Instagram users purchasing a product in the moment after seeing it on the platform.[15]

Emily Weiss, the CEO of Glossier, a direct-to-consumer start-up cosmetics company, spoke out about the importance of the public deciding what to buy and promote themselves, saying, 'Every single person is an influencer.'[16] The idea is that however many followers you have, if they like a product, they can act as an advert for it.

In the beginning, Safe 'N' Beautiful had a Facebook page, and I was constantly posting, writing blogs, working non-stop, doing the marketing and sales myself. It was marketing our products themselves. A major promotional campaign was not needed then because of the way the business was structured. We were more of a business-to-business enterprise and made many of our sales through the expos. Now this has changed, I have hired an experienced PR team to run our social media in Greece, especially Instagram, and we plan to pay key influencers to do giveaways.

---

15. Facebook IQ, 'How Instagram boosts brands and drives sales', Meta, 6 February 2019, www.facebook.com/business/news/insights/how-instagram-boosts-brands-and-drives-sales, accessed 26 May 2022

16. G Del Valle, 'Treating regular people like influencers is the key to Glossier's success', Vox, 15 January 2019, www.vox.com/the-goods/2019/1/15/18184151/glossier-emily-weiss-marketing-strategy-recode, accessed 26 May 2022

Your marketing strategy will vary depending on what your product is, but here are some promotional channels you can use:

- **Company website.** Keep it updated regularly. Ask a professional to develop SEOs to use keywords so potential customers can find your product easily.

- **Online stores.** For example, Shopify, Etsy, Amazon or Facebook.

- **Newsletter.** Ask customers to sign up to a regular newsletter so they can hear the latest updates about your product.

## Developing your brand values

Part of having a strong brand is recognising what your brand values are. These might evolve over time or you may decide them at the very beginning. Think about what you want for your brand identity. Make these values public on a website, share them with your customers, and be accountable to them.

Even now, I don't see Safe 'N' Beautiful as a traditional corporate global business, despite the fact we sell across the world. To me, it is a small independent business that puts children at the heart of it. My brand values for Snails grew from my natural instincts. I didn't want a company that operated like a hierarchy with me at the top, looking down on everyone. Everyone at Snails is very precious. Without my team, I am nothing. I treat everyone completely equally and with respect, whether they are a CEO of another company I am in talks with or the cleaner who washes out the coffee cups.

I vowed that, however successful we became, Snails would always remain an approachable, friendly company. Customers or competitors alike could always expect us to respond to their communication and at events we are the people with smiles on their faces looking to have a chat. I've never admired snobbish brands who only work with certain people or allow certain types to have access to them. I want to show that it is possible for luxurious brands to retain a sense of accessibility and fun. I am not a serious person and like to keep my sense of humour intact, even if I am talking to the head of huge global companies. I never change who I am.

I also wanted our product to be of the highest quality it could be. I didn't want to skimp on design or materials. Just because a product is for a child to play with, it doesn't mean it shouldn't be beautifully and ethically made, and that is something I strive to uphold for Snails.

At Snails, we never forget that there is only one true boss: the customer. He or she can fire everyone in the company simply by spending their money somewhere else. It's not the employers who pay the wages, it's our customers.

Another thing I am always thinking of is different quirky ways to capture our customers' and distributors' attention. We made little USBs – loaded with our company profile – in the shape of nail polish bottles, which people loved and even asked for more. I create a sense of play at our expos, too. We don't stand there seriously trying to preach about nail polish. We invite people over, talk to them and joke with them.

Eventually, after much thought, our mission and vision statements came into focus. I wanted to work collaboratively with our distributors and our manufacturers, as well as to create a wonderfully nurturing environment for my team. It turned out to be very easy to write our values down:

1. Be perfect in what we do. Be the leading premium children's cosmetic brand globally.

2. Retain steady partnerships. Create long-term relationships with distributors for the development and longevity of S'N'B's brands.

3. Make kids happy. Create a safe environment for our children to play and grow healthy.

4. Care for all women. Create green products suitable for all women.

5. Innovate. Bring exciting and exclusive new concepts to distributors and consumers.

6. Constantly improve. Constantly expand S'N'B's global network and build strong partnerships with distributors who share the same vision.

Let me tell you about one of our first distributors. Samina was born and brought up in the UK and lived in Dubai. Perhaps it was because she was also part-British, we clicked over our love of the UK and Snails. Samina went above and beyond any other distributor over the years and was passionate about her work. She was turned down for a slot in John Lewis Dubai, but didn't take no for an answer and kept returning every three months with a new sales pitch. She arranged events in malls, complete with a booth for Snails, and set up manicures. She would even pitch our product to magazines, and managed to find coverage for Snails in top-selling women's glossy magazine *Marie Claire* and one of the main newspapers in the Middle East, *Gulf News*.

Samina is an example of a distributor who was able to effectively communicate our brand values, but also believed in the product as much as I did.

## Be open to opportunities

Even if I am out of my comfort zone, I often say yes to things if someone makes me an offer. One day, I was surprised to receive an email from a tutor at the Feliciano School of Business at Montclair State University, New

Jersey, USA requesting a meeting with me. She wanted to invite her MBA students over to speak to me about Safe 'N' Beautiful, after spotting the news of our win at the Greek Export awards in 2014.

Our win at this awards ceremony had meant so much to me. Snails had been up against major companies, including Dodoni, a brand of feta cheese I grew up with and loved as a child. I couldn't believe my little company, with only six members of staff, was included alongside such an established household name. We had overcome so many difficulties exporting in the first place, as the government hadn't given us any support at all, but the award made up for it. And from it, we clearly captured attention from around the world, because even a college in America had noticed us.

I happily accepted the request for the students to visit. I had no idea what they could learn from me, but I was flattered they wanted to come all the way to Greece to find out. The meeting turned out to be great fun. I had a Q&A session on Snails, the awards and our challenges along the way. It was a pleasure to meet such enthusiastic students and I realised through speaking to them just how much I had learned over the years. The meeting came at the time we were entering the American market, too.

What I learned is that saying yes to unusual requests reaps its own reward. If you remain flexible, you can put your brand out there in whatever way possible.

## Listen to your community

Our community of regular customers is what makes Safe 'N' Beautiful products a success. When the feedback began to trickle in, telling us what people thought of our company, I really liked it. We had achieved our aim of being seen as approachable and fun, and that's exactly what I had wanted. Outsiders were also impressed by the added authenticity that I was a mother who had developed this children's product too.

But we also listened when it came to criticism. Every single email we received, whether it was from a customer, a distributor or a boutique store owner, we wrote back to with a personalised email addressing their exact concerns or comments. I never reply with generic emails.

Some of the feedback was surprising. We received many emails from Scandinavian countries asking us why we had advertised our nail varnish to 'princesses' only rather than making it a unisex product. It hadn't been our intention to make the product solely for girls, so we responded with an apology and duly removed the reference to princesses on our website.

Other feedback, often from conservative countries – like Greece, in fact – questioned us promoting beauty products to little girls, but we always responded to this in a polite, non-confrontational manner, explaining our products are suitable for both boys and girls and are designed for their development and play.

I'm always mindful that S'N'B is nothing without our global community of happy customers made up of parents and their children.

---

### CASE STUDY: SALLY DEAR, DUCKY ZEBRA

Sally Dear, the founder of the ethical children's clothing company Ducky Zebra, had firm ideas about her brand values from the start:

I have two young children and noticed how clothing had an impact on their lives. I decided to take action after my four-year-old daughter said one day, 'I can't be a taxi driver because I am a girl.'

I carried out a survey of over 1,000 parents and carers, asking them what they thought about the impact of gender stereotyping on high-street kids' clothing. Many had the same feelings as me. The clothing available in the shops gave our girls limited beliefs and unwanted messages about behaviour. After continuing my research, I discovered boys' clothing was equally problematic. The messaging on their clothes often told them to be courageous and heroic. Research shows that this stoic masculine stereotype can impact behaviour and mental health later in life.

So before I even began the company, I knew exactly what values it should have. Our clothing would:

1.  Be fun and colourful. The designs were aimed at what children would love wearing.
2.  Be free from gender stereotypes. All the clothing is unisex and aimed at both girls' and boys' tastes.

This means ditching all the stereotypes found in high-street shops.

3. Inspire kindness and confidence. The clothes all have an embroidered logo of a splash, and this is designed to remind the kids to 'splash kindness and confidence everywhere.'

4. Be slow fashion made to last. All the clothes are made to the highest environmentally friendly standards and there is a pre-loved programme for recycling garments.

5. Be made from organic cotton. This means it's healthier for the environment and the farms and workers get a better deal.

6. Create change together. We donate £1 to charity for every garment bought.

---

## QUESTIONS TO ASK YOURSELF ABOUT DEVELOPING YOUR BRAND VALUES

- What do you want your company to achieve?
- What do you want your company to add to the market?
- When a customer thinks of your product, how do you want them to feel?
- What four words are most important to you as a company?

---

# TEN
# Staying Inspired

Everyone will remember the first year their business really takes off. For Safe 'N' Beautiful, that year was 2015, when it grew by 465% on the previous year.

The turning point came when leading global publishing company Hachette asked for half a million bottles of nail polish and we had fifty days to deliver them. This was an enormous undertaking and I knew it would be a race against time to complete the order.

It was a scary experience and initially, I was out of my comfort zone. We would have to work every hour of the day, but I knew it was possible and this was an opportunity to go for. I had negotiated a deal with them to use the Snails logo on every single bottle to expand our reach.

First, I got a bank loan and bought a bottle manufacturing machine from Italy. We had to be able to bottle our own product if we were to make this order work. We also hired another floor of the office.

Next, we started working sixteen hours a day – me, my husband, Sylvie and one or two other part-time people. I spent hours hunched over, screwing on the bottle caps like crazy. By the evening, my back and neck were killing me, but every second counted. Even our accountant came upstairs to help.

The days flew by as filled bottles flew around the machine and onto the pallet. Amazingly, between us, we did it. The bottle machine paid for itself with our ability to keep up with the order. With this deal and those with our other distributors, we were selling Snails in forty-five countries by then. It was incredible.

## Keeping morale high

Not every day will be a good day. But one big factor that helps boost my own morale is being surrounded by a team of positive people. My staff can sense when I am having an off day, and they gather around to make me smile or make a cup of tea to buoy my mood.

As a leader, you also have to keep morale high for the business too. Going back to what inspired me in the very beginning has sustained me all the way through.

I cannot overestimate the importance of reading the book *The Secret*. I loved the idea of manifesting your success by visualising it, working for it and believing in it. The idea of like attracting like is very powerful.

Some of this is common sense. If you have a good energy about you, people with good energy will want to work with you. If you're bored or cranky, tired of selling, or sick of the sight of your product, that is going to put people off.

I manifested S'N'B and Snails after imagining it, believing in it and working for it. On my office door, I have the slogan 'Chief Cheerleader' in silver letters, because this is an accurate description of what my role is now. I love Snails and still believe in it as much as I did when I first started – if not more so, because I have many more products to believe in. Rather than viewing myself as a big boss, I am a cheerleader who claps along my team to turn ideas into products people want to buy. I have other fun titles for other team members, such as 'Supplies and Logistics Guru' for our supply manager, 'Account Wizard' for our accountant and 'Sales Ninja' for our sales manager.

## Whatever your idea is, make it better

There is always room for improvement, whether that's on the basic product, the marketing, the campaign or the brand. It's better to challenge yourself to improve things rather than grow complacent and stagnant. No company succeeds by believing they cannot get any better.

I learned this from reading about Steve Jobs. He continually changed and adapted, even leaving Apple and returning with more experience. Every product he brought out was an improved version of the last one.

I like to keep all our designs and products fresh and on trend. I regularly go into shops and look at what is out there on the shelves. I buy other nail products to examine the bottles, the brushes, the colours. I am the first to try new products on the market and want to stretch our brand to the maximum.

I ask my staff and customers for their opinions all the time too. People who understand and love S'N'B products know what's best for the company.

## Relax and let the ideas flow

Have you ever noticed you have your best ideas when you're walking the dog, in the shower or just about to nod off to sleep?

Scientists have proven there is a link between a hit of dopamine and creative ideas.[17] This means that, if you

17. SB Kaufman and C Gregoire, 'How to cultivate your creativity [book excerpt]', Scientific American, 1 January 2016, www .scientificamerican.com/article/how-to-cultivate-your-creativity -book-excerpt, accessed 26 May 2022

want some inspiration, you need to completely chill out and allow your subconscious, where ideas might be brewing, to come to the surface. I always keep a pad and pen nearby to jot down my ideas. After all, they do tend to pop up and disappear quite fast, however relaxed you are. Try not to force the process, but be ready and primed for when an idea does come to you.

After my burnout episode, I made myself have a holiday and relax on a sunbed for a few days. After a week or so, I found myself really switching off and even had space in my brain to think of new ideas. It was at this time that I decided we should expand our range to twenty-five different colours and increase the range to include nail art pens, stickers and glitters. I had seen cheap brands selling elsewhere and wanted to create something of better quality. By now, my daughters were also at the age where they wanted to do something a little more sophisticated with their own nails too.

In 2014, I also brought out a range of washable nail polish for women. This was because of the conversations I'd had with the Muslim women about wearing nail polish they could easily remove for praying five times a day. I designed a luxury-looking bottle, using a traditional Arabic pattern in silver to appeal to the market. The range was brought out in Dubai and was immediately copied by a rival.

Then in 2016, the French factory approached me with another fresh idea. They had created a new polish with 80% of the ingredients made from potatoes, corn and cotton – the world's first chemical-free vegan polish! The idea of this was incredibly exciting and led to the development of our S'N'BIO range.

Sometimes an opportunity arrives that you must grab. Even in this case, I didn't have an immediate sales plan or a tried-and-tested market. But I trusted my instincts. I loved the idea of a completely safe product for adults, so I ordered a few thousand bottles of this new vegetable-based product to see what would happen.

## Pivot your business

My gamble didn't pay off initially, and I struggled to find distributors for my new S'N'BIO vegan range. I began to panic. I had a lot of bottles to sell but no buyers.

I took to my sunbed for inspiration again. Relaxed in the sunshine, I let my mind wander. Once my head was clear, an idea emerged. I decided to advertise the non-toxic vegan product to pregnant women in baby stores. Few beauty products are aimed specifically at pregnant women and regular nail polish is full of harsh and toxic chemicals that some mums-to-be might want to avoid. S'N'BIO would give expectant mums peace of mind.

We created a campaign headed by a picture of a pregnant woman showing off her pretty nails. The product went on sale and within weeks the range had completely sold out!

I have never been afraid to pivot and change direction when need be. This is about making decisions to suit what is best for your business. For example, originally, I had our Snails lip gloss made in Spain. It cost the same after the custom fees as China anyway, but I thought it would be seen as a selling point for customers who wanted a European-made product. But it didn't seem to make much of a difference to consumer confidence in the product whether it was made in Spain or China, so when the delivery time was extended to four months from Spain and it would be quicker from China, I changed the production to there.

Being flexible and responding to a changing environment is good for any business. If in doubt, ask yourself, 'How can I improve my product in this situation?'

## Brace yourself for failures

It's a fact of life that not everything you touch will turn to gold. After much experience, I know out of every ten new products we bring out, only half will be a success for Safe 'N' Beautiful.

The first major failure was 'Me and Mini Me', a product designed in 2014 for both mother and daughter to paint a set of matching nails. Everyone we showed it to said,

'Wow!' They loved the concept and the design on the box. Even a competitor in France quickly brought out a copycat product in 2015.

But 'Me and Mini Me' bombed for Safe 'N' Beautiful. There were very few sales. I couldn't understand why. The feedback suggested there were not enough shades of colour – other than that, the failure was a mystery. Sometimes you're not able to understand why something has not captured the public imagination and it's best to move on and leave it behind. Something better is always around the corner.

On the bright side, during this time, I met an amazing designer through working on the 'Me and Mini Me' product called Petar, and he was able to draw exactly how I imagined things in my head. We worked together like bread and butter and I immediately employed him to help with all our subsequent designs and messaging. He understood me and Snails completely and still works for us today.

Being half British, I was always keen for my products to be sold in UK shops. But it was very challenging to find a distributor there. I had no idea why. Sometimes you hit a hurdle and there is no rhyme or reason for things to be so hard. They just are.

I have failed, and I have failed so many times before I succeeded. Don't be ashamed of your failures – they don't break you. They make you.

Ten years ago, I approached John Lewis to sell my products in-store. When they replied, I was thrilled, because back then, to receive a reply from a major store was a bonus. But despite loving our product, they explained they couldn't sell it, because we didn't sell in pounds and we didn't have a warehouse in the UK, and they didn't import from outside the UK. I sent numerous emails, begging our current UK distributor for a chance to 'prove them wrong'. We're waiting for our opportunity, and when it comes, we will grab it with both hands.

## The confidence trick

I have never had imposter syndrome, the issue you have when you don't believe you deserve success or you will be 'found out' for doing your professional job. But I understand it's something that many women struggle with.

Women who are mothers, care givers or run a household often worry the wider world will not accept us for who they are. Some of us fear we do not have the necessary skills to succeed in the business world. Some of us have to deal with the sexism that is deeply ingrained in our culture.

One time, I got accused of being 'bossy' when I asked a male employee to do a particular task. This is an accusation no man would have to deal with, I was sure.

At first I ignored it, then I confronted him. He quickly apologised. Calling out sexism is part of what women might have to deal with and if you see it, say something. In most cases, you will hear the word 'sorry' and then everyone can move on.

I want every little girl out there who has been told she is bossy to be told that she has leadership skills. Women make excellent business people. We have a great ability to multitask and our instincts around emotions and communication put us at a great advantage. I often guess what my distributors and partners want to say before they say it and can always tell them what they want to hear.

Confidence doesn't come naturally to everyone but does come to everyone with practice. For all of us, before we are a success, we have to believe we will be. Remember, if you don't believe in yourself and the product you're selling, how will you persuade anyone else to?

What will hold you back or stop people from taking you seriously is the lack of success at the very start. Money talks, and it's only when your company is established and has begun to make profit that people will stand up and take notice of you. Until then, be prepared to have to knock loudly on every door and stand up for yourself.

Trust the process. We all have good and bad days. Fear of failure is part of the human condition. Those who succeed are the ones who keep going.

# If you're a success, others will copy you

One day, one of my distributors asked me if I had heard about a new nail polish company based in France. I won't name it, but they released a product shortly after we entered the market. At first, I was horrified. I kept looking at their website, filled with worry. Would they start selling more than me? Were they going to do better than me?

The first copycat product started in Italy around 2013 and they even had the cheek to use the same bows as we did. They lasted only for a couple of years. Then the copycats grew like mushrooms. Another washable nail polish popped up in the Middle East and even one in Russia.

The old saying goes, 'Imitation is the sincerest form of flattery', and this is how I see it now. The French company is still going and they're doing OK. But we are the best-selling nail polish. We are sold in more countries, more successfully than any other. I am confident we will continue to do this.

Snails has been on the market for ten years now and is well-known as a luxury brand for kids that parents everywhere can trust. We have won over twenty awards – which isn't something you can expect, but is wonderful validation when it happens. I was also nominated as one of the forty under forty most successful business people in Greece for *Forbes* magazine.

I always tell people to be original. If you're a copycat, you can never keep up, because you're always in a passive position. You're following, not leading. Being original means you're ahead of the game.

## Keep your team inspired

The key to a happy team is a bonded team. When people trust one another, like one another and are able to laugh together, they will work hard and stick together during the ups and downs of working life.

On special occasions, I provide free drinks of a different kind (Monday is cocoa, Tuesday is coffee, Wednesday is soda, for example) and day-to-day, we often provide muffins and cakes for everyone. We celebrate every person's birthday with cake and presents and at Christmas, we have a party with karaoke. In the summer, we close for a few weeks so everyone has a proper holiday. The day before, we do a 'Flip-flop day', where everyone has a manicure and pedicure, then we take a picture of all our feet together. The essence of our company is to feel able to retain a childlike sense of fun.

I want my staff to have good memories of our company. That in itself would be an achievement. A successful company is not just about awards and turning over a profit. It's about human beings enjoying creating a product together and getting satisfaction from their work.

## CASE STUDY: SOPHIE LEAH, HOLA COCO

Sophie Leah dreamed up her own business, Hola Coco, to make a coconut hair product because she couldn't find a suitable product for her own hair. This is her story:

I came up with Hola Coco, a coconut hair conditioner product, in March 2017 with my partner, Gareth Thompson. I had been taking a strong medication for acne, which had left my hair in terrible condition. I had tried many other products and none of them worked, so I set about using kitchen-cupboard ingredients like coconut oil to make my own hair mask.

What I came up with was better than any shop version. Not only did it make my hair super soft and shiny, but unlike other products, a small amount went a long way.

I decided to set up a small company making this product and used my own skills from working in the marketing industry to promote it.

This wasn't easy. Our biggest challenge when starting Hola Coco was persuading potential customers to try our hair mask when they were already loyal to other brands and products. We had to prove our brand and tell people why it was different – and better.

We overcame this hurdle by building a portfolio of respected salon stockists who recommended our product to their clients. Over time, we built a following of loyal customers who still buy from us today.

The big turning point came when my marketing skills paid off and we managed to have Hola Coco featured in the *Daily Mail*, one of the UK's biggest selling newspapers.

It was a chance to tell our story and the response was incredible. People realised we had a quality product in a competitive market saturated with coconut hair products.

Thousands of people purchased our hair mask in one day and it took our brand to the next level. This sudden amazing interest validated my enthusiasm for what we were doing and was truly inspiring.

---

### TOP TIPS FOR STAYING INSPIRED

- Surround yourself with positive people, and keep morale high among your team too.
- Never stop improving your product or range.
- Take time to relax and let the ideas come to you.
- Don't be afraid of failure – often, it is the precursor to success.

---

# ELEVEN
# Growing A Bigger Business

One key reason for the success of Safe 'N' Beautiful products is that I know our journey is never 'finished'. It's an ongoing process of development, and I will never sit back and think, 'Oh, that's it, I am out of ideas now!'

The cosmetic industry is notoriously fast paced, with new trends coming out every season. I stay ahead of my competition, maintaining awareness of what they're doing and expanding my range where reasonable.

Over the years, we have expanded our product range to include body glitter, lip gloss shaped like a lollipop, hair chalks. We released the world's first vitamin nail polish range infused with rose water, aimed at teenagers, and an eye shadow packaged to look like a colourful cake. We removed even more chemicals from our nail polish ingredients to create a 'twelve-free' formula. This was a first among our competitors. I am constantly looking at ways to improve the formula, because there is always room for improvement. In 2022, we have bought out a new jewellery line called Charming. It's the perfect accompaniment to our nail range. We are selling in over seventy-nine countries and have beaten every prediction of yearly growth to date.

At the same time, it's important not to be too enthusiastic about growing too fast at the beginning. A company has to be able to handle the growth if they want to keep customers happy and not take on more than they can handle. For example, if you say yes to a huge order before you are ready and prepared, you might not be able to fulfil it. It's better to have fewer happy distributors than a larger number of unhappy ones. I know we could expand our distributor list further, but I am taking care to keep it manageable. Today, I employ eleven members of staff and we work effectively as a small team.

## Constant persistence is key

The only way a successful business can keep growing is by the owner's persistence. One idea I persisted with was to have a range of polish for children to match with their dolls. After the successful experience of co-branding with Hachette, I decided I wanted to find a doll company to team up with.

By 2018, we were going to the same German fair every single year. I always did well finding distributors and expanding our market there. That year, I found myself interested in Götz, a German toy manufacturer founded in Rödental in 1950. The company had such an incredible history they were even known to have inspired the classic face mould of the American Girl doll range. This make of doll was the most prestigious and luxury brand at the fair, and I was already dreaming of working with them.

I went to look for the Götz booth and was amazed to see how enormous it was. The reception alone was bigger than my entire booth. I swallowed hard and approached the receptionist. 'Could I please speak to the owner of Götz?'

She eyed me suspiciously. 'The owner is not here,' she replied. 'How may I help you?'

'I am the owner of the brand called Snails,' I explained. 'Please let her know I would love to discuss the idea of co-branding.'

She asked me to leave my business card, so I did.

I returned to our booth, crestfallen. I knew my business card would likely end up in the bin. So the next day, I returned to see the receptionist again and we had the same conversation. Once again, she asked me to leave my card. But I returned again, later that day, with our biggest and best sample kit of all our products. This time, I handed the receptionist my business card again and wrote down my booth number and my phone number.

'Please pass on this kit and ask your owner if she will kindly come and see me,' I said.

I could tell by the look on the receptionist's face she thought I was being a bit pushy. But I smiled politely and walked away, keeping my fingers crossed this would work.

My phone stayed silent, so the following day, on the last day of the expo, I went back yet again. This time, the receptionist asked me to wait a moment. Then the owner, a woman called Anke, emerged from a side entrance.

'Oh, are you the lady with the sample kit? Please tell me where your booth is. I am very busy but when I find a quiet moment, I will visit,' she promised.

I was thrilled. I returned to my booth to wait. I was so anxious that I would miss Anke's visit, I didn't even dare use the toilet all day. Then towards the afternoon, she suddenly appeared with her young daughter. Despite our small booth she looked impressed with the chandeliers we had added as a fun touch. Her daughter wanted to touch all the Snails products and I invited her to try whatever she liked.

I explained to Anke my idea of having a nail polish for dolls to match the child's. 'And I wanted to do a co-brand with the best doll on the market,' I added. Anke looked interested and thanked me.

We became friends, keeping in close touch and working together on what would eventually become 'Me and My Götz', a box with nail polish, hair chalks and make-up for both the doll and child. It became a niche, unique product for a limited edition collection.

Going straight to a big player like the owner of Götz, was something I once would never have imagined myself doing. It's very easy to be put off or to give up after a rejection. But I did it. I believed in my idea, could visualise it on the toy shelves, and decided to go for it.

However big your idea, you should go for it. Find out who could help you and ask them. What is the worst that can happen? Someone can say no. But even then, sometimes if you keep asking, they can change their minds.

Sometimes a crazy idea is worth running with, even an impulsive one. The same year I approached Götz, I spotted an advert from Hasbro, the American multinational toy company, asking for pitches for new toys.

That afternoon was quiet, so having a giggle, I sent off an application, telling them all about Snails. I forgot all about it, until weeks later, they sent me an email asking for my specific toy pitches and gave a deadline of two days.

I was absolutely gobsmacked. What had begun as a joke suddenly felt very serious. How on earth was I going to come up with an idea for a toy overnight? I began to think of games involving Snails and came up with three ideas.

I was then invited to pitch my product in person at a special event. Dimitris drove me there, while I shook with nerves. This was a once-in-a-lifetime opportunity. I knew I had next to no chance of this working, but I had to give it a shot.

I arrived at an intimidating hall, filled with a few executives, waiting to hear what I had to say. I only had sketches of my ideas and a few lines written up. I went in, sweating, hoping I didn't come across as a complete amateur.

They asked if I had made a prototype of the toy design and I almost laughed. I had had so little time to even think of anything. I made my pitch the best I could, and they thanked me.

Afterwards, I discovered that two of the ideas had been turned down, but one of them is still under consideration. Once again, my philosophy of jumping straight into a situation with two feet proved to be worthwhile.

Rejection also doesn't always have to be final. Luck and timing are also involved, and if you keep trying, eventually you could hit the jackpot. If you don't put your ideas out into the universe you definitely won't get them back, so give it a go and see what happens.

I love the quote from John Paul DeJoria, who co-founded the Paul Mitchell line of hair products. 'The difference between successful people and unsuccess-ful people is the successful people do all the things the unsuccessful people don't want to do. When ten doors are slammed in your face, go to door number eleven enthusiastically, with a smile on your face.'[18]

## Let your success do the talking

Beautiful things don't ask for attention. I've never been a show-off, nor someone who wants to brag on social media, and nor do I want Snails to.

In 2021, our product hit the shelves of the Hamleys stores in London, Abu Dhabi and Dubai, and of the iconic FAO Schwarz store in New York. In fact, the toyshops even set up a 'shop within a shop' for Snails

---

18. A Jain, *Welcome to You20.0: Your journey to your best version by discovering and achieving your dreams* (Notion Press, 2017)

measuring fifteen square feet. It looked incredibly impressive and we were reaching another segment of our target market including high-end customers and tourists.

I felt very proud. However, I didn't shout it from the rooftops. I didn't send out newsletters boasting to the world. I waited until our products had settled nicely into the stores before we released the news officially – and quietly.

I decided I would rather wait and let others in the industry find out in their own time. There is something to be said for allowing your success to speak for itself. Sometimes, there is no need to tell the world you're a success, because you're too busy being one.

Seeing Snails with its own little shop inside these famous stores took my breath away. It was another 'pinch myself' moment. But even today, I see room for improvement and growth. My excitement about what comes next never stops.

---

## CASE STUDY: NATALIE DAWSON, AWESOME BOTANICAL

Sometimes a business can grow faster than you expected. This is what happened to Natalie Dawson's homemade cosmetics business, Awesome Botanical:

During the first lockdown, I was furloughed from my father's shop-fitting company, my anxiety was running at an all-time high, and I was desperate for something to do, so I began making hand balms. I love natural scents and essential oils, so used those only. My family and friends loved them, so I decided to try selling them online.

I had to have them tested by a chemist to have the necessary documentation to make selling them online legal. I knew nothing about the cosmetics industry beforehand so it was a steep learning curve getting my head around the requirements.

I opened a shop on Etsy and called it Awesome Botanical. The word 'awesome' came from a nickname that rhymed with my surname. I made all the packaging myself and even created the logo using the design app Canva. I tried to keep it all simple to tie in with the natural theme.

The hand balms sold very fast and then one day, someone ordered thirty of them, and I jumped around my living room with excitement. I began to also make bath bombs and whipped soap. Then I made my own website via Shopify.

Within a few months, I spotted Fenwick were asking for local businesses to apply to sell in their pop-up Christmas store. I applied, thinking they would ignore me. To my amazement, they said yes. I invented a special Christmas-themed 'Ho Ho Ho' box for my range and they sold out every day.

Then I joined a Facebook group for PR and marketing companies. They asked for independent cosmetics companies to submit their products for the Top Santé bodycare products of the year. I did so, also not expecting to hear back, but they asked to try my foot balm. To my shock, they featured our product in the magazine and we were a runner-up just behind The Body Shop. It blew my mind to think I'd only started making products a few months earlier.

I was also picked by Dragon's Den's Theo Paphitis as a winner of his 'Small Business Sunday' social media slot, which attracted many more sales.

Then a customer approached me who wanted 9,300 units of hand balms to sell in a hamper. I was still making the products in my bedroom, but agreed to fulfil this order. This meant we had to rent out a unit and I had to hire family and friends to pitch in and find an employee. I can't believe I've come so far from a hobby that started in the pandemic.

---

### TOP TIPS FOR GROWING YOUR BUSINESS

- Growth is not a destination, it's a journey. The key to growth is to keep on going.
- Persistence is vital. Never stop at the first sign of rejection. Don't be afraid to try asking again.
- Take risks and follow up on your wildest dreams – they may well come true!
- Enjoy your successes and stay curious about where they'll take you next.

---

# Conclusion

I wrote this book primarily to inspire other women to start their own businesses, particularly those who want to set up their own cosmetics company. I didn't have my own 'Jeanette' to give me advice when I started Snails, but I long to help others the way that I would have liked.

## Starting your own company in just a few steps

Here I list all the actionable steps you need to take for your start-up, in chronological order. I hope you find it as helpful as I would have done.

**Step 1:** When thinking about the business you wish to create, consider:

- Your own skill set. Where do your passions lie? What products do you admire and wish to emulate?

- The information you need to take on. Research what you can and learn everything about what you want to do. Almost anything is teachable via YouTube, blogs, books and articles.

- Where the profit lies. Look at what other companies have done successfully and how they have made their money.

**Step 2:** Understand your product's unique selling point. Does it solve a problem? Does it fill a gap in the market? What is different about it from the competing products out there? Identify what your competing products are doing and see if you can think of something different.

**Step 3:** Do a test run. Can you make prototypes of your product? Can you test products out at home on family and friends? Who will help you make your product if you're outsourcing it? Can you order a small amount to trial it? Ask for feedback every step of the way. Early feedback on early editions of your products is vital.

**Step 4:** Decide on your target market. Is it mums? Kids? Both? All sexes? A certain demographic? People who are ecologically minded? This is very important, because it will determine how you communicate your brand, such as what language you use in the copywriting, what packaging you choose.

**Step 5:** Nail your brand. What are you going to call it? How will it appeal to your audience? Writing down a few 'typical' customers and their characters can help you visualise the kind of people who will be buying it.

Consider the brand as a whole. This includes the use of colours, language, fonts, logos. Keep these consistent across all packaging and communication channels. Find a designer whose style you admire and work closely with them if you can afford this. Also consider what values you would like your company and brand to fulfil. It's a lot to consider, but many of the answers to these questions will be solved on your research journey.

**Step 6:** Understand where you need to reach your audience. I knew I had to sell Snails in pharmacies or mid-range stores to begin with, and I needed distributors to help with this. Where will you advertise – Instagram? Facebook? Magazines? Other channels? Think about what social media channels your target market uses.

**Step 7:** Nail your domains and trademarks. Once you have decided on your product and market, think about the brand name and take the steps to protect them. Buy the domains in different countries and trademark the name early on. Use a local lawyer and online companies – there's no need to make this an expensive endeavour.

**Step 8:** Work out the finances. Do this as soon as possible. I had $50,000 and that was for everything, including travelling and paying to attend the expos. Make a list of your costs and be absolutely rigorous about including everything.

If you need a bank loan, look into the offers from different banks. Ask other SMEs for advice. Only take on debt you can afford to pay back quickly.

**Step 9:** Understand what your limitations are. What is it you don't know? Can you learn from the internet or do you not have the time or the skill set? I had many tasks I could learn to do myself, such as marketing or approaching distributors, but I realised I needed to outsource other things like website and packaging design, because I needed a professional.

**Step 10:** Make a website. Never skimp on this. Pay a professional to do it if necessary. It has to look extremely good, as it's your first shop window. Develop an online presence early on. Make it easy for early customers to buy your product.

**Step 11: Register your product.** You will need to take steps to have your cosmetic product tested for safety and quality and make sure that it is registered before selling to the public. There are a number of stages to this depending on where you are based:

- First, you will need to get a CE certificate. This proves your product is safe to sell and specialised pharmacies can test the product.

- The country where you live will have its own rules and regulations for registering your product.

  - In the USA, the relevant body is called the FDA (the Food and Drug Administration).

  - In Europe and the UK, you can ask a registered chemist to help with the registration of your product. They will deal with the admin such as test reports, safety assessments, etc.

  - In Europe, you will need to register your product with the Cosmetic Products Notification Portal (CPNP), which is a free online notification system created for the implementation of Cosmetics Regulation (EC) No 1223/2009. When a product has been notified to the CPNP, there is no need for any further notification at national level within the EU.

  - In the UK, you need to register your product with the Office for Product Safety and Standards. All the steps are included on the Office for Product Safety and Standards website: www.gov.uk/guidance/making-cosmetic-products-available-to-consumers-in-great-britain

**Step 12:** Decide on the countries you wish to export to. You can hire a web researcher to make a list of stores that could potentially sell your products. This will save you a lot of time doing your own tedious research.

**Step 13:** Target one country at a time. Choose a researcher who is from this country, ideally, or who speaks the language fluently. Ask them to compile a list of email addresses, websites and telephone numbers for specific distributors. If they send you an Excel document, you can easily export the contacts to your email server or other platforms. But remember, never send bulk emails. Always send to individuals, using their correct names and titles.

If a department store tells you to use their generic email address, always ask for someone specific. Nobody responds to generic (usually info@) email addresses, unless they are a small boutique. If the researcher is struggling to find the exact names, ask them to look on LinkedIn and find the buyer's direct email address.

**Step 14:** Overcome the language barrier. When approaching foreign distributors, always send an email in their first language. Pay for a translator rather than using online translation tools straight away. If you're short of money, use a translator for the initial email, then continue the communication using translation software, asking for forgiveness for your poor language. This worked for me in the early days. Often, people also speak English, so this isn't a problem for many.

**Step 15:** Find distributors via similar brands. Check company websites for the page 'Where to find us', and find the stores or distributors that sell their products. If they are in a similar product category as yours, reach out and contact their distributor.

**Step 16:** The best way to find a distributor is via face-to-face meetings at expos. Make a list of the expos you would like to target and consider where your products fit in. For example, is your product niche? Is it for the vegan or eco-friendly market? Or is your main market children? Is it high-end or low-end?

Attending the appropriate expo is key to finding your best buyers. Think back to who your consumer is and where they will shop. Key expos for my market included those in Dubai, Germany and the LUXE PACK expo in Monaco. Check the website https://tradefest.io /en/tag/cosmetics for lists of expos you could attend.

**Step 17:** Make professional and beautiful sample kits. Do not skimp on the quality for this. Use full-sized products. We thought up creative ways of illustrating our products – for example, we made a 'Story of Snails', which looked like a book, with the products neatly displayed inside. The USB stick shaped like a bottle of nail polish had all our company details stored on it for potential buyers to look at in their own time.

Make your sales kit eye-catching, accessible and easy to understand. Working with a good designer will help with this. Make sure they land in the hands of the appropriate people. Send your samples directly to a named person.

**Step 18:** Open an Amazon store. If you need help, research online or ask a professional. You will need to include bar codes for all products and include SEO keywords for customers to find you and improve the rankings. Shopify is another popular online shop service.

**Step 19:** Visualise your success as you go along. Try to do this every day. I take time out to read inspiring books to boost my mood if I am feeling a bit flat or defeated. My colleagues also help refresh my positive outlook on a daily basis. Find out what works to refresh your enthusiasm and keep doing it.

There will be times of tiredness, exhaustion and mental fatigue where you'll need that boost. Practise self-care regularly, so you can keep yourself topped up.

**Step 20:** Keep on top of trends. Look carefully at what the market is doing. Is a new innovation overtaking? Could you grow in other areas? What can you afford to extend to?

We refresh our ranges every year and extend them when we think there's scope. Don't be afraid to bring out more products. Some will fail, but some will succeed.

**Step 21:** Invite lots of feedback from customers. We include a special area on the website to invite opinions from members of the public, and we read and respond to every single one. I can tell when a product will be popular thanks to this insight. I never forget that without our customers, there is no Snails.

**Step 22:** Think big but don't get big-headed. You might win an award or get picked as a best product, but don't let your success change anything. The best businesses nurture their creative ideas and keep growing. We were born to be real, not to be perfect.

**Step 23:** Keep an open heart at the centre of your business. My close relationships with my staff make it all worthwhile for Snails. My door is always open for them, and I want them to feel safe when communicating both good and bad comments about the way things are operating. If your staff feel secure in their relationship with you, any problems can be solved faster. I also care about my staff and customers, because without them, Safe 'N' Beautiful and Snails don't exist.

When I began my journey with Safe 'N' Beautiful, I had no idea where it would take me. I dreamed of Snails becoming the Chanel of the children's nail polish world and I believed in it enough to try, but the reality was that I had no idea what to expect. What started as a business idea to help support my family through a bad patch is now a product that's conquered markets around the globe.

Starting a business is not for the faint-hearted. There will always be unexpected challenges and frustrating difficulties along the way. At times, it will feel almost impossible to keep going, but no road to success is linear. It's only those who can hold their heads high and maintain a steadfast belief in their product who will make it. The real story behind the success of Snails is one of carrying on against all odds.

Whatever your business is and whatever your circumstances, it's possible to attract back what you put out into the world. May you enjoy the journey as much as I have.

# Further Reading

Please see below a list of books that have inspired me along the way, and I hope they do the same for you:

Sophia Amoruso, *#GIRLBOSS* (Penguin, 2015)

Rhonda Byrne, *The Secret* (Simon & Schuster, 2008)

Malcolm Gladwell, *Outliers: The story of success* (Penguin, 2009)

Tenzin Gyatso, His Holiness the 14th Dalai Lama, *Be Inspired* (Hampton Roads Publishing Company, 2019)

Maria Hatzistefanis, *How to Be an Overnight Success: Making it in business* (Ebury Press, 2017)

Walter Isaacson, *Steve Jobs: The exclusive biography* (Abacus, 2015)

Vex King, *Good Vibes, Good Life: How self-love is the key to unlocking your greatness* (Hay House UK, 2018)

Idowu Koyenikan, *Wealth for All: Living a life of success at the edge of your ability* (Grandeur Touch, 2016)

JP Lash, *Helen and Teacher: The story of Helen Keller and Anne Sullivan Macy* (Delacorte Press/Seymour Lawrence, 1980)

Robin Sharma, *The Monk Who Sold His Ferrari* (Harper Thorsons, 2015)

# Acknowledgements

Thank you to my husband Dimitris, who believed in my crazy idea from day one – although he did give me funny looks in the early days when I was flying with enthusiasm. Without you standing by my side, I wouldn't have made it.

Thank you to my daughters, who thankfully don't hate Snails anymore! Thank you for your patience, understanding and cheerleading on the way. You both have always made me want to keep going.

Thank you to my team, who support me every day and make Safe 'N' Beautiful the success that it is. A business is never about one person – it's always about the team behind the scenes.

Thank you to Shannon Kyle for being patient with me when helping me to write this book.

Thank you to my father and stepmother, who helped to look after my kids while I was busy with Snails. Without them, I wouldn't be here today.

Finally, I want to finish with the quotes from my walls in my meeting room:

'Listen to your dreams – they are smarter than you are.'

'If you want something you've never had, then you've got to do something you've never done.'

'Believe that good things will happen and then they will.'

# The Author

Jeanette Sklivanou was born in Newcastle Upon Tyne, UK. She is half British and half Greek. She is the mother of two beloved daughters, Valerie and Georgette.

In 2011, she launched Safe 'N' Beautiful, creating safe, non-toxic products including her most popular: Snails nail polish. Fast forward ten years and the Snails brand is a global success, selling in seventy-nine different countries. Jeanette has donated to many causes, raised money for Cambridge Breast Cancer Research Unit, EAC Network (child abuse prevention), is a member of PETA and supports many other organisations.

She has been featured in *Fortune* as one of the forty most successful Greek entrepreneurs under forty. Her drive is to create smiles on the faces of children all around the world.

🌐 www.safe-nails.com
🔗 www.linkedin.com/in/jeanettesklivanou
📷 @jeanette_sklivanou